REVELATION

REVELATION

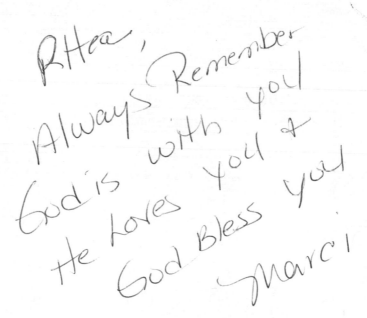

Rhea,
Always Remember
God is with you!
He Loves you! &
God Bless you!
Marci

Marsellas Coates

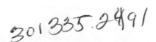

To order additional copies of this book, contact:
Xlibris
1-888-795-4274
www.Xlibris.com
Orders@Xlibris.com
724354

CONTENTS

To God, my Heavenly Father, who loves me;

Jesus, my Savior, who taught me how to love;

the Holy Spirit, who guides me in that love;

and

my Mom, who taught me about the Lord.

ACKNOWLEDGMENTS

. . . *To all those who have loved me just because,*

. . . *To all those who have supported me in my endeavors,*

. . . *To all those who have given me inspiration in spite of,*

You all know who you are,

Thank you.

MERCY

"For all have sinned and fallen short of the glory of God."
--Romans 3:23

"For I will be merciful to their unrighteousness, and their sins and their lawless deeds, I will remember no more."
-- Hebrews 8:12

GRACE

"For sin shall not have dominion over you, for you are not under law but under grace."
--Romans 6:14

"For by grace you have been saved through faith, and that not of yourselves; it is the gift of God."
--Ephesians 2:8

LOVE

"If God is for us, who can be against us"
--Romans 8:31

"Nor height nor depth, nor any other created thing, shall be able to separate us from the love of God which is in Christ Jesus our Lord."
--Romans 8:39

"As God has allowed me to come to know myself and know the things of my heart, that I can see my life and understand this life from the places in my heart that bring love behind them; instead of seeing life from the places that has affected my emotional state. Not from the place of anger or disappointment or guilt, but God allowing me to know Him from a place of love and acceptance and salvation . . .

"The thankfulness I possess for this Grace from God has afforded me the ability to accept the things I cannot change, the courage to change the things I can, and the wisdom to know the difference. Living one day at a time; enjoying one moment at a time; accepting hardships as the pathway to peace; taking as He did this sinful world as it is, not as I would have it; trusting that He will make all things right if I surrender to His will, so that I may be reasonably happy in this life and supremely happy with Him forever."

Marsellas Coates

THE BEST-LAID PLANS

Revelation and the progression of it, as God intended it to be, have set my life on a path that has brought me to this point of understanding.

At this stage of reflection, seeing how God revealed himself to me during the course of my life has turned into what I now see as a constant. Yes, I constantly see the revelation of God's love, direction, provision, and protection, as it has carried me throughout my life. It was only because of what I considered great failures that I would even consider the search of why I was getting it so wrong. I was constantly questioning myself and wondering why there always seemed to be a shadow cast over my endeavors.

From the outside looking in, it had to look as if I was living the life with all the bells and whistles; all the while, my internal struggles and convictions forced my life decisions. Although I blamed a few people for why I had taken some of the paths that I had chosen for myself, it was only upon this most recent revelation of who I am in Christ Jesus that I have had to deal with my own ugly truths of why I had been failing so much and so greatly. With hindsight looming over me at this age and with life's experiences teaching me God's lessons, my ugly truths have taken on a new meaning. *"For My thoughts are not your thoughts, Nor are your ways My ways,' says the Lord, 'For as the heavens are higher than the earth, So are My ways higher than your ways, And My thoughts than your thoughts"* --Isaiah 55:8–9

In my life, as I've pondered what it was that God wanted from me, oftentimes superficially asking the Lord what it was He wanted, I remained fearful that if I asked too sincerely, He would actually respond in a way I was not ready for nor willing to acknowledge yet. This state of being left me unwilling to commune with Him and unwilling to live the life set out before me by Him. But despite all that I was apprehensive about, He never stopped blessing me, and I never refused any blessing bestowed upon me.

After learning that all the plans that I had laid out for myself served only what was best for me and that they served no purpose in glorifying God, I had to find out exactly what it was that God wanted me to know about who I am and who He is. **Was it a true failure on my part or a directional path laid out by God?** It was questions such as this that remained unanswered as I went on with my life, which left me with a constant and ever-present feeling that there was something between me and God that I had been ignoring far too long. I needed to know what it was He either wanted from me or was saying to me.

As time went on, I questioned, "Why would You bless me in ways such as these?" placing myself immediately in a position to feel unworthy of His blessings. He knew how fearful I was of living life every day set out by Him, feeling I could never live up to it anyway. He knew where my life was, which was far away from His Glory, and He also knew how I had been disobedient toward Him.

However, I deeply wanted to be obedient to God's way of life, but life's presentations were saying something totally different. My heart was feeling one way, but my determination was saying something else. Life was telling me that I did not need to wait on Him and that I could have things the way I wanted. It manifested itself in such a way that I believed that I could have what I wanted when I wanted it—right now if I wanted it—even if I had to do whatever I needed to do to get it for myself, believing the fallacy that I had been hearing from others, such as "God helps those who help themselves," which is not even in the Bible. This left me in a perpetual state of inner turmoil, believing, Why should I bother God? He's already busy. I could get if for myself. *"The eyes of the Lord are on the righteous, And His ears are open to their cry"*--Psalm 34:15. Was I supposed to rely on Him for all of my needs? *"And my God shall supply all Your need according to His riches in glory by Christ Jesus"* --Philippians 4:19 How could He and/or why would He possibly want anything from me, knowing what state I was in? *"The Spirit of truth, whom the world cannot receive, because it neither sees Him nor knows Him; but you know Him, for He dwells with you and will be in you"* --John 14:17

I could not go on any longer living life like this. I had to find the answers. I needed to know if this was the life I was supposed to live and, if it wasn't, how could I get myself out of this state of mind and of the despair my heart had been feeling. I did not know where to begin to look or even how to display a path to right living, as each time I did, I found myself with yet another situation taking my time and attention away from a settled place with the Lord. There always seemed to be another something I needed to address, add my two cents to, or give my direction to resolution. So I started with the only thing I knew—me—and I wasn't too sure who that was, except to know that I felt beaten down, broken, tired, and a host of other descriptions for any given day or circumstance. I had to do something; it was do-or-die time. Distinctively, I began reflecting on what it was my life had offered me, what it was God had revealed to me about my life thus far. And so here we are, a reflection of that revelation.

* * * *

Seeing Life. It has certainly been a life lived at both ends of a few spectrums—from the spectrum of not knowing how things worked naturally to the spectrum obtaining the knowledge of how things worked through Christ Jesus, from the spectrum of loving the only way I knew how to the spectrum of learning how to love in Christ Jesus, from the spectrum of not caring about people to the spectrum of loving my neighbor as myself, and finally, from the spectrum of understanding things as I saw them to the opposing spectrum of living in the light of the Lord and walking with God. *"For the flesh lusts against the Spirit, and the Spirit against the flesh; and these are contrary to one another, so that you do not do the things that you wish"* --Galatians 5:17

As I've always desired to write the things that were given to me by the Lord, not truly understanding what it all meant, it was with much trepidation that I began to do as such. I felt I was holding in all this information that would save me from myself, yet I was unable to convey it to anyone or even to myself in my own thought processes. I was, in grand fashion, living a paranoid life, judging everyone and everything for their worth to me. While wanting to express my thoughts pen to paper, this paranoia left me apprehensively willing to put any thought on paper, anguishing that it would be the most uninhibited thing I could do. Knowing all the while I was willing to judge, I was unwilling to be judged by the very objects of my judgment, living fearfully that it would open me up to criticisms of my core beliefs that I just was not ready to explain or defend.

I was living with a lifelong void as well as the unwillingness to express myself, which left me far removed from a place of inner peace. The fallacy was living as though I knew what the void was because it oftentimes posed itself as the trillion-dollar question. It was a wondrous awaking to finally come to the knowledge of what that void really was. It was me coming to the knowledge of the grace and truth of Jesus Christ. *"For the law was given through Moses, but grace and truth came through Jesus Christ"* --John 1:17 It was through that grace and truth that I came to a point of realization, and that was that I needed to actively seek to fulfill the spiritual desires within me, and that meant taking care of that void.

As well I can imagine, most people have identified what their voids are and some maybe not so much. But isn't it the search of fulfillment for those missing parts of ourselves that we've labeled as voids that we do the every day for, the get out of bed, the reason we do this thing we call life? Bearing to resolve that we have unanswered questions that we pose to ourselves, aren't we seeking answers with logic, fact, claim, truth, or whatever we may wish to call it? We are looking for the purpose, whether it be openly or not so openly.

Admittedly, when you are full and satisfied with answered questions, you really don't feel the need to nor do you want to move from the comfort zone of knowledge and belief within yourself. It's that place that you've deemed a sufficient place that you find you are able to live with yourself and your life's decisions.

I reflect on times throughout my life that I've had intimate moments with the Lord, either through prayer, verbal discussions, or whining, unsatisfied that He would not allow me to have my way or begging my way through some desire or questioning Him about some lack of understanding on my part. And just as suddenly as the day begins every day, I realized that I woke up one of those days with a uniquely different outlook on life. And as uniquely different and strange as it was to others around me, it was even stranger to me. I couldn't begin to tell those I knew just how obscurely I saw the same things they were looking at, even if it was obvious. Nothing I saw was remotely close to how others had perceived it. What had God done to me? What had He done to my perception? *"Therefore, if anyone is in Christ, he is a new creation; old things have passed away; behold, all things have become new"* --2 Corinthians 5:17

But I was clear on one thing: I knew in my heart all I really wanted was for Jesus not to leave me here when he returns for his church. *"One thing I have desired of the Lord, That will I seek: That I may dwell in the house of the Lord All the days of my life, To behold the beauty of the Lord, And to inquire in His temple"* --Psalm 27:4 I cannot express in any words how important this is to me, even though in my mind's eye, I had given importance to some things here on this earth, reconciling within myself that what my heart wanted and what my mind saw were two different things. *"Hope deferred makes the heart sick, But when the desire comes, it is a tree of life"* --Proverbs 13:12

Now clearly acknowledging the gift from God was that He sent His Son and that through Him All might be saved—*"For God so loved the world that He gave His only begotten Son, that whoever believes in Him should not perish but have everlasting life"* --John 3:16—and bearing in mind that reconciliation to the Father is only through the Son—*"Jesus said to him, 'I am the way, the truth, and the life. No one comes to the Father except through Me'"* --John 14:6—I knew I didn't stand a chance on my own merit(s).

It is now through more recent understanding and revelation that my focus and desires have changed. My heart said, speaking through pain, "Why should I care about this world? This world doesn't care about me." And my mind said selfishly, "Look out for your own self. No one is going to do it for you." Gratefully, through Christ Jesus, that has turned into loving my God with all my heart, my mind, and my soul and loving my neighbor as myself as Matthew 22:37 and 39 proclaim, *"Jesus said to him, 'You shall love the Lord your God with all your heart, with all your soul, and with all your mind.' And the second is like it: 'You shall love your neighbor as yourself.'"* So in the meantime and in between time— actually all the time— coming to share the knowledge of this gift from God, my outlook has taken on a different precedence.

Acknowledging that I am overwhelmed at the acceptance of my life, my situation and just how blessed I am brings joy to my soul, knowing that this life has been such a beautiful gift, the present that God gives me every day, a new day. Even at my lowest, bringing to remembrance that Jesus makes all things new and telling myself that I needed to learn how to put one foot in front of the other and not drag the past along with me and that I am a new creation through Christ and I am not the old any longer, it all is my carrot in front of the horse. It is exactly what I had been chasing after. My void has now been filled.

So at this point in my understanding, I just really wanted to share my thoughts on it, so here it is—my *life* as I see it and live it, the Gift from God.

THE FAMILY WAY

My Beginning . . . Where God determined my place in His plan is where my journey began. My life, this beautiful gift from God, has allowed me to see my truth by learning from His truth, my life experiences all through the eyes and perspective given to me. It is indescribable. *Gift* is defined as "something given voluntarily without payment in return, as to show favor toward someone, honor an occasion, or make a gesture of assistance; present," and this is how I have chosen to see my life—a gift from God. Imparting His spirit to dwell within me, it is Him who I see in my life every day with everything. It is this perspective that helps me stay connected in direction and desire and reminds me that He has blessed me with daily new mercies and that those mercies only come from Him loving me. So each day is another opportunity to be obedient and remain in service to the Lord. *"I beseech you therefore, brethren, by the mercies of God, that you present your bodies a living sacrifice, holy, acceptable to God, which is your reasonable service"* --Romans 12:1

But I clearly did not start with that point of view. Oftentimes feeling like my viewpoint was derived from a far more sinister and nefarious place, it was a viewpoint I'll describe as a different state of mind, a mind-set taken from the foundational base of my childhood rearing. I found I was perplexingly mesmerized about Jesus from a very young age, always internally aware and conscious of God even before the formal introduction. I was inwardly conscious of Him but never had a full grasp of the hows or the whys and even the wherefores, just this feeling that He was a part of me, as I was me. It felt like the "who" that I was. The awareness of His existence stayed with me as I grew; it grew in my spirit and consciousness. *"For in it the righteousness of God is revealed from faith to faith; as it is written"* -- Romans 1:17 It was the knowing that God was always with me. *"For He Himself has said, 'I will never leave you nor forsake you'"* --Hebrews 13:5. Now whether I conferred with Him about anything, that's a different story altogether.

* * * *

Family. With the adage being "You can't choose your family," I was always privy to family madness and mess; and despite the hardships of an averagely normal dysfunctional childhood, bearing all the scars that came with that dysfunction—the feelings of abandonment, family secrets, severe family discord, displacement, abuse, and character assassination—I managed with survival skills. I marched through life as a young child living with what appeared to be horse blinders on, unsure whether I put them on or whether they too were a gift from God. I wore them as if they were an outer shell, covering me from the arrows of defeat. Yet they served as protection from what could have been a number of deathly situations. Never reconciling whether my outlook on it was a choice of mine or not, this outlook was affecting, but its effects on me were visibly and differently received by me. In another version, the minutia just did not seem to affect my direction as it did other family members. And even shorter, I just didn't care. Being internally more emphatic for those who lived with the same discord, my demeanor oftentimes displayed an air of disdain. But overall, I guess you had to have some sense of self; otherwise, you could have found yourself easily dissuaded.

How do you survive with insurmountable odds against you? It certainly is not an easy thing to do. I disguised myself, never letting anyone in. I wore the happy faces to get me through whatever event I was present for. Although those disguises covered pain, I wore them as badges from battle. They protected my sense of worth. They helped me smile when there was clearly nothing to smile about.

Recently, my mother sent me a photograph of myself as a baby, when I was maybe eight months old. I see myself sitting there, staring at whoever is taking the picture, as I am contemplating the look on my face, wondering, "What was I thinking at that time, or what was I seeing and hearing at that time?" because the look on my face seems to reflect how I felt growing up—perplexed. It sort of surrounds that saying that your mom would say to you as a kid: "If you keep making that face, your face is going to get stuck like that." Did I know something then? Had God whispered something to me that left me with the ability to just sit back and watch how things played out? *"Even there Your hand shall lead me, And Your right hand shall hold me"* --Psalm 139:10.

My origin was anything other than a normal, textbook family life. It did not consist of a mother and a father who had 2.5 kids with a cat, a dog, or maybe even a goldfish. No, my beginning was far from that. Using the vernacular "suspect," the conditions were unusual—a mother who had an extremely difficult time at things; an absentee father who claims he didn't even know I existed; given the surname of a man who married my mother, who wasn't my father, and subsequently, the name wasn't his either; and reared with an extended family, which struggled to maintain family unity. Whew! What's up with that, Lord? Was God revealing Himself to me from my beginning, affording me the ability to bear witness to His protection and direction? *"He who dwells in the secret place of the Most High Shall abide under the shadow of the Almighty. I will say of the Lord, 'He is my refuge and my fortress; My God, in Him I will trust'"* --Psalm 91:1–2.

Viewing my life from what was normal to me, it showed itself to be anything but. So there I was, this little girl in this big world, starting out with a unique set of circumstances already stacked against me. It was me possessing a unique beginning, accompanied by insurmountable odds, leaving me with the ability to see life from a different perspective. Oftentimes presenting itself as feelings of isolation, it was where I had been placed. It was my life, my family. It was the only way of life I knew—hard.

Looking back and remembering all the family discord, I just couldn't reconcile why there was so much of it or why the family unity seemed to be grouped or gone. What purpose did God have in placing me here? I bore witness to much of it without explanation. I spent a good deal of time trying to figure out the anger; all the while, God had been protecting me from battles that could have been detrimental to my growth. How could this way of life bring Him glory?

It became clear to me that God had placed me exactly where I was supposed to be. *"O God, You have taught me from my youth; And to this day I declare Your wondrous works"* --Psalm 71:17. The lessons of God's family were similarly shown in my family. He was showing me exactly who He is, just as He did His own family, meaning, as with His family, He subjected them to discipline; He protected them, directed them, and provided for them. *"Blessed be the God and Father of our Lord Jesus Christ, who has blessed us with every spiritual blessing in the heavenly places in Christ, just as He chose us in Him before the foundation of the world, that we should be holy and without blame before Him in love, having predestined us to adoption as sons by Jesus Christ to Himself, according to the good pleasure of His will, to the praise of the glory of His grace, by which He made us accepted in the Beloved. In Him we have redemption through His blood, the forgiveness of sins, according to the riches of His grace which He made to abound toward us in all wisdom and prudence, having made known to us the mystery of His will, according to His good pleasure which He purposed in Himself, that in the dispensation of the fullness of the times He might gather together in one all things in Christ, both which are in heaven and which are on earth—in Him. In Him also we have obtained an inheritance, being predestined according to the purpose of Him who works all things according to the counsel of His will, that we who first trusted in Christ should be to the praise of His glory. In Him you also trusted, after you heard the word of truth, the gospel of your salvation; in whom also, having believed, you were sealed with the Holy Spirit of promise, who is the guarantee of our inheritance until the redemption of the purchased possession, to the praise of His glory"* --Ephesians 1:3–14. And that all is for His Glory.

The time I spent trying to figure things out left me with little time for anything else. Acknowledging very few friendships or relationships, it became the test for survival for me. Duck and roll; bob and weave. Make sure you know where the next meal was coming from, and prepare for the worse. My family was not the first family to go through discord, as many have survived unhealthy blaming, shaming, and ostracizing; but I was dealing with feelings of where to fit in. It was painful and perplexing. Why would anyone want to fit in with discord?

This was my family, the only family I knew. The constant shifting of living here and living there also made things a little crazy. It easily left the good times questionable. Questioning how and why I was feeling this way left me wondering about the people I was placed around. What were the lessons to be taught from them? It all felt deliberate, out of my hands, like God did it on purpose, leaving me with no say-so. Leaving me without one person around me whom I could talk to about it, I began to develop an anger within me. And why should I be angry about something God had done for me?

Everyone seemed to be in their own world, engrossed with what was wrong with everyone else. It was society as a whole hating one another. It was very disheartening, to say the least. I cried a lot, inside and out.

Looking back, what was God showing me because all this couldn't have been for nothing? What was he revealing to me in my youth that would be added to my development, and what was He protecting me from while allowing me to grow in the midst of chaos?

Coming to the acceptance that this was the life God had for me encompassed my thoughts about human nature very deeply. I began to question everything—why people lived like this, why people treated each other with such hatred, why God allowed me to witness all of this, even why He allowed things to transpire the way they did. And to top it off, why would they want me to believe that it was my normal? Simultaneously, there was also something deep inside of me pushing me, urging me, with great passion, to look at it with separation. Whatever it was, it was delivering urgency for me to view things with the perspective that it was not my stop in life. I was not to get used to this way of living. Was it God's direction showing itself? Was it Him who made me see that this world of people I was intertwined with and these places I was subjected to were not my resting place, that I needed to focus on preparing myself for what was in store for me and not concern myself with what was going on here? *"And in that day there shall be a Root of Jesse, Who shall stand as a banner to the people; For the Gentiles shall seek Him, And His resting place shall be glorious"*--Isaiah 11:10. It was so powerful within me that I could almost hardly imagine anything else. I was watching myself in a movie, waiting for it to unfold right before my eyes.

As the Bible conveys, there are many within the family of God who have suffered the same fate. So my life's circumstances are nothing new, only new to me. With awareness of God presenting himself to me at such an early age, inherently a part of me, I just came to believe it was the way it was supposed to take place. It came along with me when I was born. *"For You formed my inward parts; You covered me in my mother's womb"* --Psalm 139:13. He allowed me to navigate this minefield while coming to see that life wasn't the perfect picture I had imagined in my head. It was the knowing that I felt special to God and that He was always with me. It was the most complete feeling I've ever lived with. He did not let me rest on it, even though it comforted me, protected me, and settled me.

Conversely, as if bearing witness and dealing with it all wasn't bad enough, there was also an even more terrifying aspect lurking about me, daring me to believe that I was unwanted. This led to such things as feeling unloved, that I was in the way, and that I was being used as a means of continual animosity. The two forces within me challenged me to choose which way I was supposed to go. If I had chosen to believe that I was unwanted and unloved, then I was doomed to stay within that space, continually seeking the approval and love of those who surrounded me, all the while wondering where my place was within it; or I could live with the opposing view and believe God would make a difference in my life and that I should not settle just for what was handed to me, that I should follow what I truly believed was right for me.

* * * *

Born and raised mostly in Philadelphia, looking at it as my home wasn't as special as I would have liked it to feel. Don't get me wrong, I love my home; but seeing it as that was almost tantamount to me looking at Camden, New Jersey, as somewhat of a home as well, since I've spent time living there too. The transition from Philly to Jersey came as a result of just moving around so much. Remembering the difficulties that we faced as a family just became a part of my everyday life. There was always something new to deal with, and sometimes we just had to move on with our lives somewhere else. Wherever we moved though, it was home. My mom placed emphasis on making any place we lived as our home.

"She," my mother, was having such a hard time that it caused a sorrow in me, which I felt deep to my core. I saw the makings of sadness grow over her, which I could do nothing about. I watched her face some difficult struggles with family, as well as obstacles and adversities from making her own life's decisions, but I also have been blessed to see her overcome some of those choices and adversities. She taught me about the Lord. We learned early who Jesus was. Memorizing Bible verses was just part of my rearing.

And it was those few verses that I carried with me throughout my life. Nonetheless, it all had taken a toll on her, as well as her children. I began to look at my mother, other family members, and people in general under different lights; some lights were bright, and some lights were dim. It was almost as if life separated itself and put them into individual categories just for my understanding. Was God developing my sense of awareness of people who were or were not following Him? Was God giving me the picture of what it looked like to be separated from Him?

What seemed most important was the one home I knew as stable was my grandmother's house, and that grew increasingly divided, and almost with dire urgency, I needed to remain connected to it. I couldn't understand it. Why could I not let this side of my world go? It was a topsy-turvy existence. How it hurt my mother so when I continued going there when her struggle there had been so great. I wasn't sure why, but I saw the anguish in her face as I went for visits or even sometimes when I stayed longer than I was supposed to. It was the closest thing to a fixed residence that I had known. It didn't move, but we always had to, given whatever circumstance or drama my mother had to attend to at that time. Sometimes I knew it was easier for her when I stayed at my grandmother's house, just because she had to deal with so many of life's emergencies, and there were always quite a few. So while there, she knew where I was and that I was safe, and she didn't have to worry about me while her attention was drawn elsewhere. But I knew she suffered each time she had to relinquish those moments with me. And I myself knew that it was sometimes better when I stayed there because I knew I had meals and shelter. Placement, yes, my placement; although it demonstrated signs of weakness and doubt within me, there was God's handprint ever-present and evident, showing His intended plan for me.

There were times when I so hated hearing and seeing what was happening between family members, seeing how great their struggle was. Just observing all that had been going on around me, it was oftentimes best just to stay out of the way. This arose in me the question, where do I belong? I hated the discord with an unbelievable passion, always asking myself, how can people treat each other this way?

The feelings of having limited options of where I stayed or even what I was to do with myself felt like a black plague of sorts. I was here, and I was there, but all I knew was I did not belong anywhere. I didn't feel like I belonged with my mother; there was no father that I could turn to and family who I think just kind of took pity on me. I wondered why should my first remembrance of feeling anything be sadness when a part of me, deep down on the inside of me, felt a joy in the middle of all of it. What was that about? I just couldn't put the puzzle pieces together. It all seemed like a manipulated choice. Conversely, I can only imagine how they saw things, as I am certain they were living with their own set of truths.

So I lived with this perception, forced to have an out-of-body view on it because it just didn't seem like it was right, like it was real. This couldn't be my life. Was I dead already and looking at myself from some other place, yelling at myself, "Can't you see what's happening here? This really isn't your life! *Run!*"? Frustrating as it was, it was my reality. Yet there was the love. Why couldn't I love them hard enough that they would love all those around them. How I so desperately wanted their love, needed their love, and needed them to love one another. The feeling of despair flooded my senses, and life just seemed so unfair. I constantly questioned God why things were this way.

Had I known how much my Heavenly Father had his hands on me, I certainly would not have troubled my spirit with those feelings. Looking back, I now know that my Heavenly Father had placed me in this life with this family for a reason. There was no figuring it out then or even having a clue that He had planned it that way for me. My thoughts were on other things. It turned out to be vital in my development for the lessons that God wanted me to know about Him, in learning to depend on Him and not anyone else. It was Him showing His great love for me. He began showing me what He looked like, without me realizing it was Him. Still, even knowing all that, I never left my position of anger and feelings that this was not the place for me, that I belonged in another place. It was the self-importance I gave myself at a young age that forced me to grow up seeing things other than what God had intended, and it was my lesson to learn. All I could see before me was the fact that I was safe.

I would look at my mother through such loving eyes, observing her, studying her with such intensity. I could see her stress, and I wondered why life presented itself to her in this way. Why was I wondering these things about my mother? What was God doing for her that He wanted me to observe and learn from? Just how did it all work with this family of mine, the family that I did not feel part of? But even that had its place within God's plan.

Watching my world was awesome, confusing, and frustrating. There was so much happening around me. The setup was in place, and I had to live through it. I wasn't sure how it was going to turn out and come to fruition or even when, but I knew I had to wait to find out. So here we go.

LIVING JUST ENOUGH
FOR THE CITY

City life was not easy. You had to learn how to navigate through it so you wouldn't get entrapped by the snares of it. And my grandmother, who's namesake I am, was a formidable woman, knowing that as you grow in life, you learn lots of things; some things you keep, some you don't, some you apply as a means to progress, others you may use as a standard for living. She and my mother were forever doling out words of wisdom. The lessons learned from my mother and grandmother always surrounded lessons from the Lord, which encompassed kindness toward people, living right, and respect—you know, the things Jesus taught us, how we should be toward one another. *"Therefore, whatever you want men to do to you, do also to them"* --Matthew 7:12. You know, *the Golden Rule:* "Do unto others as you would have them do unto you." Some of those things taught to me I held as my standard for my living. And then there were sayings that I just wondered to myself, what in the world were they talking about? I did not know what they meant then, but with growth, they have meaning.

Now with all these pearls of wisdom bestowed upon me, I went along trying to live within the means provided, under the circumstances. Sometimes you experience life by watching it pass you by, and sometimes you're so engrossed in it, and you can't escape the path of its ugliness. No matter how pleasant your thoughts are around a particular experience, you will inevitably encounter some insanity, which perpetuates and fuels the path of someone's determination for your success or demise. This is where, as a young child, the Lord has covered me with his grace. *Your sticks and stones could not break my bones nor could your names hurt me because I know who I am, a child of the Almighty King.* So what we had to counter it with was church. Yes, it was just a fact of life. There was no escaping it. City life in the '60s and '70s, there was only one thing on Sunday mornings, and that was going to church.

No matter whose house I found myself at, we always had to attend church. My grandmother attended a Methodist church, while my mom attended Pentecostal churches. Wherever I was, there was the obligation to go. Nonnegotiable. *"Train up a child in the way he should go, And when he is old he will not depart from it"* --Proverbs 22:6.

Spending time at my grandmother's house, which was a small two-bedroom row house, there was not much room, but there were more than enough people to occupy every inch of it. There were always more people than space. Going through life and taking with me the lessons from living in this type of environment were valuable as well as costly, some of which I'm still paying a price for. Having thrust upon me the value of lessons learned, it pricked my sensitivities to caution and awareness. Urban living during this time was certainly not the easiest place to be. It was a time of gang wars, race riots, making it above the limits of impoverished living, and picking and/or choosing sides. Either you followed the path of social acceptances or you made your way into the path for your life. *"Enter by the narrow gate; for wide is the gate and broad is the way that leads to destruction, and there are many who go in by it. Because narrow is the gate and difficult is the way which leads to life, and there are few who find it"* --Matthew 7:13–14.

I was always surrounded by someone, anyone, everyone from the inside of the house as well as the outside. My head was swimming with ideas of my surroundings, and my eyes were overwhelmed with what I was seeing. It just all seemed to be way too much for any one way of life, and most seemed to settle within it. People always seemed to have somewhere to go or something to do but never seemed to be getting anything done because the environment never changed. It was a cultural thing, a sign of the times, with all the same hearts and minds there indulging.

It was the roller coaster of daily living, demonstrating a constant reminder of how unstable my life was. See, when you go to five elementary schools in six years, you tend to feel as if there is no place for you, and you end up in survival mode and you take the best out of life where you can get it.

I really don't remember when all the moving started, but my mother at one point moved us into a house in the Mount Airy section of Philly. It was a beautiful house. We would run throughout it with such freedom, without a care in the world. But it was a house that left painful scars. As with a good majority of mothers who worked, my mother worked as well, sometimes leaving us to our own imaginations, and our imaginations ran wild. And with examples being galore, I have chosen to share just a few, certain ones that I've deemed significant to my development in bringing me closer to my walk with Christ.

My sister and I would run throughout the house carefree and with reckless abandon. And it was there that my sister ran through a glass door, turned around and slammed the door in front of me; I pushed my hand right through the glass. There was so much blood that I thought I had cut some of my fingers off. I had never seen that much blood in my short life. It was terrifying. Once again, God revealed himself to me through healing in that next door lived a nurse, who fortunately was home at the time and was able to pull extremely large chunks of glass out of my hand, right where my fingers connected to my palm, therefore saving my fingers. I almost lost three fingers in that incident. Little did I know that my fingers would play such a major role in my life. I wasn't even ten years of age yet.

* * * *

Set in Stone. Thinking about living under some set-in-stone conditions and how it took on a form of its own, etching its way through whatever aspect of life it rendered helpless, and remembering how I had to go along with others as life's events took shape, it always was a bad place for me. It was a constant reminder that I was the tagalong. Everyone there was with someone who wanted them there; I was there not to be left at home alone. I would endeavor to be connected but always tried to hide the emotional state I found myself in as I participated. If you were to look at my face, still carrying around that same look from my baby picture, you certainly couldn't tell how I felt on the inside because I wore my battle masks. Never—and I mean never—let them see you sweat. Scrounging through those years put a lump in my throat.

What happened to my adolescence? Was this its emotional demise? It was a time when I felt so many different emotions while so many things were happening to me all at once. Wasn't I supposed to be a kid, running around, playing games with my friends, along with the constant learning of what it was to develop into a young lady? I felt like it was a setup, just as if my Salvation got together; God the Father, Jesus, my Savior and the Holy Spirit made a plan for my life and set me in motion, led me through the pitfalls, only to guide me right back to reconciliation with my Heavenly Father. I had the hookup, and I didn't even know to what degree this Holy Trinity had my back. It was set in stone, but the hits just kept on coming.

* * * *

In the Eye of the Storm. It was in my prepubescence or in puberty years when I had the experience that would allow me to witness God's mercy and protection of me, leaving no doubt, for it was through his wondrous love for me that I am still here to even tell the story. It was in the time when running to the corner store, at any hour, was safe. There was no one out, plus everyone knew you. On a visit to my grandmother's house, I was playing cards with my cousin, who was a few years older than I was, when it was bestowed upon me to run to the store at ten-thirty at night to get potato chips. I was the youngest, so why was I chosen to go to the store? It was my destiny to see God's protection for my life. So I slipped my shoes on, folding the heel over as to turn them into slides, and I slid on up to the corner store. Now this corner store was owned by a man who was known for his demeanor toward people and his cheesesteaks. To some people, he was very nice, and yet there were others who he held a strong hand with. As he was also known for keeping this shotgun leaning against the counter for everyone to see.

As a neighborhood, we all grew up with this store, running in and out of it to buy snacks, play pinball, or just hang out a bit, as it was a comfortable position for us to know our way around the store. So on this particular run for potato chips, I entered the store and did not see the owner or his shotgun leaning against the counter, but there was a steak burning on the grill. I started to yell for him, "Mr. X, your steak is burning!"

As God did not allow me to go too far into the store, except to attempt to move the steak and stop it from burning, I proceeded to go behind the counter for that purpose; and that's when I saw him, Mr. X, lying there in an extremely large pool of blood with a green trash bag loosely sprawled over him as to attempt to cover him. I froze. It was at that exact moment when two guys came from the back of the store and said, "Mr. X is closed," both holding guns in their hands. It was at that time that I could literally feel God's hand grab the top of my head as He so gently turned me around and pointed me in the direction of the front door. *"Though I walk in the midst of trouble, You will revive me; You will stretch out Your hand Against the wrath of my enemies, And Your right hand will save me"* --Psalm 138:7.

I really do not remember feeling myself whole at that moment. I was truly living the poem "Footprints." It became clear to me that I was unable to assist in my own survival. Terrified inside myself, it was as if the Lord etched in my spirit, ***"The times when you have seen only one set of footprints is when I carried you."*** It was because of His protection that I even made it out of the store alive. His gentle kindness barred me from any harm. And so we all proceeded out of the store. One of the men walked out in front of me, me in the middle and the other man behind me. It was but for the grace of God, there I went.

As with many small streets in Philly, there were alleys that led to the back of the row houses, and so we exited the store, leaving Mr. X still lying on the floor, the steak still burning on the grill, me and the two killers accompanying me out. If we had been leaving footprints in the sand, you surely would have seen only two sets of prints, and neither were mine because I was being carried on the wings of my Father. *"Surely He shall deliver you from the snare of the fowler And from the perilous pestilence. He shall cover you with His feathers, And under His wings you shall take refuge; His truth shall be your shield and buckler. You shall not be afraid of the terror by night, Nor of the arrow that flies by day, Nor of the pestilence that walks in darkness, Nor of the destruction that lays waste at noonday"* --Psalm 91:3–6. One man ducked into the alley and went behind the houses, and the other one walked me all the way down the street, I'm sure to know where I lived.

I could have died any number of times throughout that ordeal, but obviously, my Savior, as He reigns, had plans for my life that I was unaware of, and neither did the two men know of.

As I reached my grandmother's house, I turned to look at him, and he nodded at me as to give some sort of signal that I was supposed to acknowledge. I didn't have a clue what it meant. Was he going to come back and kill me too? Did he just want to know where I lived in case? So here was the weirdest part of all of it; it felt like he was walking me home to make sure nothing happened to me, almost in a protective state. Was he grateful that I hadn't screamed or made a scene, alerting someone to what was happening? If he had only known, I couldn't open my mouth even if I wanted to. I wasn't even in my own body. I don't know who was there in my place, keeping me at bay from reacting as we walked together down the street, but I just kept quiet and continued to walk home. Oddly enough, I only felt afraid because of the situation. I felt protected.

I got back inside the house, and my cousin, seeing the look on my face, said, "What's the matter with you? Ooh, Mommy, something's wrong with her!" screaming out to my grandmother. I couldn't speak. I just remember trying to voice something, anything. All I could say was "I . . . I . . . I . . . I . . . I . . . Mr. X is dead." My grandmother went into immediate action. As my aunts were screaming at me—"What happened? What happened?"—my grandmother said, "Get her upstairs, and lock her in my room." By this time, someone must have alerted the police because it was shortly thereafter that they arrived. Everyone went to see what happened. My grandmother and my eldest aunt came upstairs to find out what I knew. As I was telling them, through cries and tears, that he was lying dead on the floor behind the counter and crying, "They saw me. They saw me. I walked out with them. One of them walked me home," this is when my grandmother grabbed me and hugged me so tight, I remember being swallowed up by her. I cried so long. It was one of the rare moments in my life that I had ever seen my grandmother lock her bedroom door because she locked me in.

I remember peeking out the window and hearing all the sirens. Everybody came out to see what happened. And I guess my family went to see if anyone had seen me, and yes, someone had. A man who lived across from the steak shop told the police that a little girl who lived in the middle of the block had seen who did it. I remember the detectives knocking on the door and my grandmother telling them, "No one in this house has seen anything," and that was sort of true. I was so scared; if asked, I couldn't tell you who was there.

As we walked back to the corner, I stood by my aunt, almost hiding behind her, shaking like a leaf being blown by the wind, watching what I knew everybody else wanted to know. It took her feeling me shaking, as I held on to her, to say, "Take her back home. She's not able to be up here." The next day my grandmother sent me back to New Jersey, and I couldn't come back for a very long while.

That event changed my life. It has been amazing that, in my life, it was never brought up to me again. For those who knew I knew, they never told anyone I knew. I guess it was the code of the streets. And I went on living my life as if nothing ever happened, only to have this memory to share with two others. I'm sure it changed their lives as well—three lives, never to be the same, bonded by tragedy but connected through God.

* * * *

You Gotta Keep on Truckin'. After this extreme life event, amazingly, God dimmed the memory as His plan for my life took an even more direct turn. I was never so determined to make it, in my limited capacity of knowing what making it was. Those feelings of spending a great deal of time alone surprisingly invigorated me to compete with myself to see if I could top every task placed before me. It was partly for the daily dealing with life's challenges that turned into the driving force that I used as a springboard. I would challenge myself that I could give better than I was getting. What fueled me was the thought that I might have to lean on someone for anything. And with vigor, I was propelled to make the point to myself that I needed to make it without them. *"Trust in the Lord with all your heart, And lean not on your own understanding; In all your ways acknowledge Him, And He shall direct your paths"* --Proverbs 3:5–6.

Instead, God had opened a door for me, which had afforded me to see, yet again, that this was not my stopping point in life. I was to learn from these hardships and live with the intent to do something with the blessings from them. I was not to use it as a weapon to rise myself above those whom I desired nothing more than not to be like. But it was the desire to get out of my circumstance that grew in me that far outweighed the ability to see what was being given to me.

It was like a switch had turned on inside of me. I had convinced myself that I was never going back to the feelings of inadequacy again. Although God never meant for me to rely on self, He didn't give up on me. *"In God is my salvation and my glory; The rock of my strength, And my refuge, is in God"* --Psalm 62:7. He keeps me covered in protection from all the surroundings in my life. And as life presented itself, I seemingly took off as if God had put wings on my back and said, "Go fly, my child. I will carry you through this plan I have set for you." Feeling like I no longer needed anyone's permission or approval for my existence, I hid those feelings deep inside of me and covered them with the look of disdain for most of mankind. It was a trick perpetrated upon me by the enemy of my spiritual life, to look down on where I was. But I was no better. I was in the same boat as everyone else here. And we all were in the boat with Peter, needing to stay focused on the Lord to keep us from sinking, which we were all doing rapidly. *"And Peter answered Him and said, 'Lord, if it is You, command me to come to You on the water.' So He said, 'Come.' And when Peter had come down out of the boat, he walked on the water to go to Jesus. But when he saw that the wind was boisterous, he was afraid; and beginning to sink he cried out, saying, 'Lord, save me!' And immediately Jesus stretched out His hand and caught him, and said to him, 'O you of little faith, why did you doubt?'"* --Matthew 14:28–31.

While I was deciding my fate, God's plan for me was going on around me. So with the commuting back and forth from Camden, New Jersey, to Philly practically every weekend, it had sent me into a tailspin of what I considered as my home. I just wasn't sure of either place.

Starting middle school came with all adolescence issues. There was the desire to be accepted by those around me. I saw it as a nuance to engage in a ritual that only caused insecurities. I just didn't see myself that way. I saw myself with a purpose, and making a whole bunch of friends was not one of the things that was important to me. Once again, this was not where I was going to be, so why even bother? My childhood had taught me coldness, separation, and nonacceptance. It was a nasty battle, and I did not want to be in that headspace or emotional space. Knowing that I had anger toward my surroundings, my heart was telling me to love, but my surroundings were saying something else, and I took it personally. It was saying in an extremely loud voice, "Get out!"

However, knowing God is the Creator of heaven and earth, *Elohim*, and that he created man, hence creating me, I naturally didn't make the connection to all this favor I was experiencing and that it was from my Heavenly Father. It was for God, opening hearts toward me, that I had been receiving favor. When you go through life wondering why for so many reasons, you question any favor toward you. Why it would come your way? But as I grew and God continued to reveal his favor toward me, I didn't feel the need to question it. It was just given, and I just took it. I knew I started with nothing, acquired nothing, and managed to have what I needed to survive; and that had to come from the favor of the Lord. *"Indeed now, your servant has found favor in your sight, and you have increased your mercy which you have shown me by saving my life; but I cannot escape to the mountains, lest some evil overtake me and I die"* -- Genesis 19:19.

And for the two years of summer jobs I had, I saved whatever I could, helped whoever I could, and just lived with what I thought was from my own effort. It was what was keeping me, sustaining me—so I thought. God has always revealed himself to me throughout my endeavors, all the while I insisted it was me.

As my life seemed to be this never-ending circle of where was I living now, I always had to adapt for school, friends, and churches and always wondering how I would fit in. I had to adapt to living in Philly and going to school in New Jersey. It seemed to be rough living wherever we went. In my middle school years, it seemed particularly harsh.

It was in my seventh and eighth years of school that I was living in New Jersey but traveling back to Philly for what to me was stable living. It was because of the harsh life that I found myself needing to feel safe and stable once again. We lived without electricity, gas, and water for a time. I used to have to do my homework on the porch before the sun went down. I was always leaping right into the action of survival.

It was one day as I was waiting for the bus to go to Philly when my teacher drove by me and stopped, asking, "What are you doing, and where are you going?" To my surprise, I answered her truthfully without hesitation, "I'm going to my grandmother's house in Philly." Somewhere in my eighth grade, I had been catching the bus to go across the Benjamin Franklin Bridge into Philly and then riding another trolley just to get to my grandmother's house. It didn't occur to me that whatever I said to her could have ended up in a bad situation for my mother. But since my mother was having a difficult time with her own troubles, I just claimed to have been heading to my grandmother's house for the weekend. She never questioned me about my mother or why I was so young traveling to Philly by myself. But without hesitation, she opened her heart and her car door and said, "Get in. I'll drop you off since I don't live far from there." It was a Godsend. The Lord sent a chariot for my delivery. The inside of me burst into tears. Why would she do this for me? I couldn't let her know how much it meant to me at that time. Money was short, and I constantly had to juggle: do I eat with it in New Jersey, or do I get to Philly with it, eat for the weekend, and possibly get more money?

Once again, God had revealed himself to me in such a miraculous way. How she could have gotten into trouble transporting a student across state lines. And without truly knowing what kind of person she was, I got in her car and took the ride. It was trust and faith for both of us. No one knew, and we didn't mention it in school. But on Fridays, she would ask me if I was going to Philly, and either I would say yes and she would say, "I'm leaving at four-thirty," or I would say, "Not this weekend." She never questioned my motives except to ask me who lived in Philly and that I was good company for her on her trip home. She was a very sweet teacher, very loving and caring as if it was just her nature. I was looking at God in her and didn't even know it. And that went on for my entire eighth year. Then summer came, and I graduated to high school and didn't see her anymore. She was always very pleasant and very easy to talk to, one of the many angels God placed in my life.

When I had to move back to Philly because my mom took ill, I was still enrolled in the New Jersey public school system. So as I graduated from the eighth grade to the ninth and started high school, I had to travel on three buses to get to school every day.

I had to take one bus to get me to the bus that took me over the bridge, and once over the bridge, I took another bus that took me to my school. It was real cool for a while, as the other kids had no clue that that was my trek every day. I guess they thought I got on the bus at the first stop since I was always on the bus when they got on.

* * * *

Work Makes the World Go Around. Having a couple of summer jobs with a summer youth program was my first opportunity to earn for myself. I felt so empowered with living. Not having to ask for permission to be me, it was the best thing I had ever known about myself. It told me it was okay not to have to ask anyone for anything in the form of money for survival's sake. *Hallelujah!* The beginning of the connection being broken. Life took on a new meaning for me. I could finally get on with my life and not look at how I was feeling. I can finally work on what it would take to get away and not look back. All I saw was my future, and it was away from the maddening cries of this current existence.

While I was earning income for myself, things were changing in my homelife. I found myself staying in Philly more and more. Since I was working there, people I called my friends were there, and not being alone was there, I just continued to travel to school in New Jersey and work in Philly and began to line myself up with this place as my home again. Yep, New Jersey was coming to an end.

Finally, the day came that my mother was sick and tired of what I was doing as she had never waned in her relentless banter, relaying her feelings about what was going on in Philly, why I was there, and me not going over there anymore. She was all over the place. So as time went on with the continuation of my trek back and forth from Philly to Jersey and Jersey to Philly, I guess my mother had had enough. Her response to how she was feeling about it and/or what she was dealing with because of it was clear and solid.

It became one of the saddest days of my life. We had discussed and argued about my still going to Philly to my grandmother's house and me not wanting to be in New Jersey. But what she didn't know was that my working meant more to me than being in a place where I was alone or was constantly hearing anyone's displeasure on the state of things. I had one thing on my mind, and that was working so I could move away from these crazy people, all of them. Living a lifetime of hearing people bicker will do that to you.

I do not think people consider what they teach children by their actions. Intent is one thing, but actual living is another. That is why Jesus came, taught, and died so we could stop messing each other up. What my family never knew was as much as I wanted to love and help them, I equally wanted to get away from them. Learning how to treat other people was one thing; learning how to treat one another was something totally different.

It was a day like any other day when, out of the blue, in a voice my mother hailed at me angrily and disgusted; she said to pack some of my things and that she was dropping me off at my sister's house. I don't even remember feeling anything about it; I just did it. It was cold and unfeeling. As we drove up to the apartment complex of my sister and her then-boyfriend, I remember my mother continually, with nonstop frequency, telling me how much of a disappointment things were for her and who had equal footing into how things turned out. She pulled up to the curb, leaned across me, opened the door, and told me to go live with my sister. I remember standing on the curb with my one lowly suitcase, watching her drive away. Her last words to me were "I'll be in touch. I'll call you." She drove away without even giving me a second glance. I turned and walked up to my sister's door and knocked. She opened the door, and I said, "Mom just dropped me off."

As I tried to control whatever emotions I had at that time, the situation became completely uncontrollable, and we argued and fought that night. I had to call my aunt to come and pick me up as she had done so many times before. So there I was, back in Philly again, for good.

* * * *

So here we go again; another ordeal that sent me into overdrive. I just had to get away. Was it life sending me down this path, or could it have been on purpose? What was it that I needed to do to get away from the madness in my life? And with nowhere else to go, I jumped into full gear.

So around in my eleventh grade of school, with an alternative school program, it offered the opportunity to attend a regular school part of the day and to attend a vocational school the other part of the day. It was brand-new. So I signed up for the tour, and it was on that tour that I first saw something that would change my life to my given profession, stenography. It was like magic; my hands touched the machine, and the machine felt my fingers. It was marriage, so I said, "I do." I loved it. It was the first thing that challenged my mind. It afforded me an opportunity to see things more distinctively. Life was presenting to me a real goal, a tangible goal, a challenging goal, one that I would put my fingers on literally, right now, those same fingers that were saved by the Lord. So I embarked again with another thing I could concur. It was where I was supposed to be. Things were starting to take shape. However, I never forgot my original desired goal, the United States Marine Corps. I had to be seventeen to enlist, and my mother had to sign for me to go in, but she was gone, and I wasn't seventeen yet.

I had seen my uncle come home from the Marines in his Dress Blues, and I knew I had to have those. "How do I get some of those?" I asked my uncle. And while touching my nose with the tip of his finger, he ever so gently said, "You'll have to be a Marine to get these." I was fourteen. My mark was set, and all I needed was "get ready" and "go," and I was off, off to become a United States Marine, no matter what it took.

But it was around my sixteenth birthday that major changes started to happen for me. I had had a couple of different jobs by this time—the usual Mickie D's, Burger King, having it my way—but I knew I didn't want to stay in fast food. Although I always ate and gave away food to my family and friends, I knew I had to move on from there, or it was going to be my forever. I could not become content with the status quo. My initiative was fueled by desire, disgust, and need. It was because of the inward battle to be better than my circumstance that I had decided that, whatever I needed to do or whatever it was God wanted me to know, it was time. And the Lord's favor continued. It was in my junior year of high school, which was an all-girls school, that I wanted a new job. So being offered the work/study program, I jumped on it, anything to make more money so I could be one more step closer to out. The program was leading, and I followed. I had gotten an interview with the director for the Northeast Region of the Peace Corps. I had no idea what the job entailed except some clerical things, and with no background except typing classes from high school, I took the slip and went down for the interview.

As I took myself downtown for the interview, I had not placed value on what importance the job would have on my life going forward or just how much it would change things for me. I didn't even put together that I would be competing with other people for the job. I remember going with the thought, *Wow, I'm moving on with my life,* not *Would I get the job?* My brain didn't even process the process. I had such boldness about myself then. It turned into a movie right off of TV. I couldn't have made it up if I wanted to.

The boldness of my demeanor told me the job was mine, but the reality was I walked into the office, and there were about six or seven other girls that were already there, waiting and sitting there in their Catholic school uniforms, and then there was me. I remember the disgust on my face and asking myself, *What am I doing here?* and *What would make me think I could get this job over these girls?* My ego was deflated, and how my demeanor quickly changed, but I sat there anyway. It was storybook.

As we all sat in this long hallway, I was on the end chair. I could hear them talking as if they all knew each other, never saying a word to me. They sat there as if it was a shoo-in for one of them, ignoring me with such snide demeanor the whole time. They all went in one at a time; I was last. Then it was my turn. So I walked in with the sense of self-protection. I knew I didn't have it, but I wasn't going to run out and give anyone the satisfaction of seeing me sweat. I walked in, and there was a lady at a desk.

She asked my name, I handed her the slip of paper from school, and the interview commenced. And at the end of the interview, she told me I had the job. I could have cried. I was so bold in my thinking then that I asked her outright, "Why would you hire me over all those Catholic school girls?" and she said so lovingly, "You seem like you really want the job and would work hard at it, and that's what I need." I was in like Flint.

I think I cried all the way home. No more hamburgers. No more silly people working my nerves about who was more together than the next or the rest. I was out of there, never to look back. I saw it as a sense of superiority coupled with gratefulness. But it was those hamburgers and fries that kept food in my mouth, money in my pocket, and a few friends by my side. Yes, I was forever grateful, but it was time to let that life go. And so I did, not looking back and not keeping in touch. Done.

As I started the next chapter in my life, the plans I had were starting to take shape. Had I acknowledged God in my blessing? I think at some minimalistic level I had, looking up and pointing my finger as I had done so many times before and saying, "Thank you, Lord. Good looking out." I was now about to see people working in the "real world," separate and apart from the younger people I had been working with. It wasn't as if I had never seen adult people work, but it was seeing adult people do adult things without complaint to me, just people coming to work every day, grateful for a job, and doing what needed to be done. It was a lesson taught straight from my Heavenly Father. It was something only seen on TV and never in my world of unsurety, all supplied through angels sent from heaven, set to assist in my delivery back to my Father, Abba Father. *"And He said, "Abba, Father, all things are possible for You. Take this cup away from Me; nevertheless, not what I will, but what You will"* --Mark 14:36.

I was making even more money at every job than the last. So much so that I told my employer, because of my school hours and credits, that I would be able to work whenever I wanted, that I had enough credits to graduate, and that I was just waiting for June to do it. It was the first step to my own demise. I hadn't asked or spoken to anyone about the choice to self-destruct; I just did it. They never questioned it, and I just kept on working, making more and more money, so eventually, I stopped going to school altogether. I had two months left to graduate and said, "What the heck. I can do this for a living." It was one of my dumbest ideas to date. Yes, I dropped out of high school with two months to graduation. I know, I know, stupid is as stupid does. And I kept working at a part-time job, mind you. Such arrogance I possessed.

So when I wanted to continue on with my job, since they kept me for the summer, the job was supposed to be available for the next semester. How was I going to stay? I had to tell them that I was no longer in school. I never thought the plan through. But with all things working themselves out or God forcing my issues into His plan, I enrolled in another school in Philly, another alternative school. *"And we know that all things work together for good to those who love God, to those who are the called according to His purpose. For whom He foreknew, He also predestined to be conformed to the image of His Son, that He might be the firstborn among many brethren. Moreover whom He predestined, these He also called; whom He called, these He also justified; and whom He justified, these He also glorified"* --(Romans 8:28–30. I would only need to go to school for six months, enough time to acquire the missed hours from the previous year and actually return in June to graduate.

And I would not go back to a school where I had to repeat a grade, not me. Not "Ms. I-got-a-job-working- for-the-Peace-Corps-and-you-don't." The humility came over me like a shock wave. I did not want anyone to know I had to repeat the twelfth grade for one credit, not academics but for one credit—attendance. Yes, I was ashamed, but it didn't stop me from working.

Getting ready for my graduation, I remember my grandmother was so proud, although I didn't truly believe it. Why I didn't believe it I really did not know. What I knew to believe, through countless examples, was marred with disbelief. I was graduating from high school, a year later than I should have been, but I did it nonetheless. It was weird but exhilarating at the same time. I had my coworkers from the Peace Corps there sitting in the middle, cheering me on; I had extended family sitting on the right side, cheering me on; and I wasn't sure if my mom was coming, as it was always difficult to reach her, but when I did, she said she wasn't sure. Although I lived with the uncertainty of her coming, I was glad when she managed to make it.

And so I graduated from high school, feeling accomplished. But let's not forget where we are and who we are because immediately upon accepting my diploma, my mom left. I wasn't even off the stage. What could she have been still suffering with? It was heartbreaking not to be able to help her. It was just a feeling that I had become all too familiar with. I could not see the pain in her because I was too busy looking at my own pain. I just shook it off and kept going.

DADDY'S LITTLE GIRL

Abba Father. Aramaic, translated as "daddy." *"But as many as received Him, to them He gave the right to become children of God, to those who believe in His name: who were born, not of blood, nor of the will of the flesh, nor of the will of man, but of God"* --John 1:12–13. *"When my father and my mother forsake me, then the Lord will take care of me"* --Psalm 27:10. Growing up, what never seemed to cross my mind was the thought of me having a father. What an odd statement to say. I was too busy trying to survive. With him not there and never spoken of, I ultimately took the position of a mongrel, cast from a lot of kids that no one wanted, just taken out of the pile, unclaimed freight. I was fourteen when my mother told me who my father was, briefly saying it at the kitchen table and never speaking of it again. *And so she thought.*

Never being able to process emotions associated with events, what I became was someone who had the ability to keep it moving. Having to process all that life was offering me was too much to bear, so why think on it? I questioned, once again, was it another virtue that God had blessed me with, or was it just my disgust? *"Rejoicing in hope, patient in tribulation, continuing steadfastly in prayer"* --Romans 12:12. So I just kept it moving.

The realization is children really only rely on what is told to them. What my mother said to me came out so obscurely; it didn't have meaning. She said it in passing, producing no evidence and no body. What was she saying to me, that I had my very own father? What did that mean? I had no clue, nor did I have time to figure it out. Clearly not a topic of conversation and dismissed of its own importance, I learned to do the same thing.

What does it mean to grow up without a father? *"Without father, without mother, without genealogy, having neither beginning of days nor end of life, but made like the Son of God"* --Hebrews 7:3. It's a perplexing question, which can yield a myriad of responses. What did God intend my father to be to me, to impart to me, to bequeath to me? Could it have been just simply the love of a father to a daughter? Or have we given up on fathers? It's a question best answered by the beholder or the lack thereof.

As we grow, it becomes increasingly more difficult to separate ourselves from our desire. However, it is the sound doctrine of Christ Jesus that forms the basis for the attachment. In our Father (and father), we trust. *"If you had known Me, you would have known My Father also; and from now on you know Him and have seen Him'"* --John 14:7. So God, my Father, blessing me as He always did, allowed me to understand this missing part of my life. Demonstrating His love for me ever-presently, with all things coming to light, it was through an unfortunate set of circumstances that I came through the process. As a family, such as we always did, congregating in the dining room was the norm, and it was through a conversation that the truth emerged.

It being summer in the city, one relentingly hot day, as it was my practice to always sit and listen, the conversation landed on fathers. And it was through insensitivity that I found out that I had a relative closer than I could imagine. Surprisingly, a little more than twelve blocks away were the makings of my connection to my father. I found myself watching my world unfold. The Lord began to pull the cover off hidden emotions that I dared not tackle. I wasn't prepared to deal with this, nor was I emotionally capable to respond to it. So there I was, face to face with my reality, feeling like I'm twelve years old, afraid to face the next two minutes. I had turned eighteen the prior year and, to my own credit, had accomplished a few things for myself, but I was stuck, frozen, and confused. Here we go again. Those in control of my destiny, and I could not come to my own defense. How could these people have this information for me and not give it to me? Was it God's will for me not to know until now?

Acknowledging my presence with a "Hi, sweetie, I'm your cousin," all I could do was stand there and say hi. I had to look visibly nauseous because I could have just thrown up. Who are these people? What kind of people would do this? Was I just some "nothing" that it wouldn't matter to them that I had feelings? Was their position as the information keeper more important than me knowing who my father was? Shocking, completely shocking. I felt as if I was again a stranger in my own body. All I could tell myself was that I meant absolutely nothing to these people, and I let the anger set in. My whole perspective on life changed.

This man, my cousin, picked up the phone, and the next few words spoken haunt me to this day. As he's dialing the phone, it starts to come to me; he knows who my dad is. How dare they! I'm ready to curse out loud at this point, but God was holding me tight at this moment. I could feel Him protecting my psyche, my mind, but I was about to blow. I felt Him telling me to just hold still one more moment. The swell of anger in me could have blown like I was Mount St. Helens. I couldn't even process the concept of what was happening; my brain had switched off.

Knowing that he was holding the telephone, waiting for an answer, all I could do was stand there helpless. I remember him saying, "It's me, man. You ain't going to believe this, but —— is here, and she has your daughter. Yeah, she looks just like you. You can't deny this, man. She looks like you spit her out . . ." So I'm standing there, melting into a puddle of worthless crap. I thought I knew hate from anger but not until that moment. I erased the word "trust" out of my vocabulary right then and there. I'm not sure how they saw me, but I knew how I saw them. And after more conversations between these adults, who treated me as if I wasn't even in the room, still maintaining informational control over me, we left. The rest of the day was a blur. I can't even remember if there was a conversation about what had just happened, but I'm sure there was. I was in total shock and just sick to my stomach over what had just taken place.

The next couple of weeks went on as if that dramatic scene didn't unfold. I went to work, and I went to school, and I came home—yeah, home, my grandmother's house, with these same people who had been participating culprits in withholding information from me that could have and would have changed my life, depriving me of what was rightfully mine—the connection to my dad. There were so many more questions to ponder. Now I had a father. tangible. Where has he been all this time? I was so sick of the question game, especially since gaining some semblance of direction for myself and working on my plan for departure, I certainly did not want to be here again, having more questions that went unanswered.

Lord, what are you doing to me? Why so much of it? Was he using my life as some test model? What could He possibly want me to know about who He is, as my God, in this situation? How could this bring Him glory? *"For it was fitting for Him, for whom are all things and by whom are all things, in bringing many sons to glory, to make the captain of their salvation perfect through sufferings"* --Hebrews 2:10.

Then the day came that I would meet him, my father. As it was on another summer day, not too long after the "you can't deny her" conversation, I had come home from work as any other day and headed into the dining room to speak, which was customary and expected because of the manners taught to us. You don't come into the house and not speak to whoever is home. And there she was, my grandmother sitting at the table, and she was not alone. So I spoke and proceeded to excuse myself to head upstairs, and just as I was about to leave the room, she said, "Wait a minute, baby, this is your father." I froze. "Oh, hi" was all I could muster out of my mouth," and he spoke. I don't even remember what he said. All I could do was look at him as I said to myself, *So this is who I came from? It's about time you showed up. Who are you, and where have you been?* The questions just flooded my mind as I stood there looking as stupid as the word *stupid* is. I couldn't imagine what was going through his mind either, but I just didn't even care. And in an attempt to save me from myself, my grandmother said, "Why don't the two of you go into the living room and talk?" And so we did.

As we sat across from one another, stunned, while searching for the "do I look like this person," him looking at me and me looking at him—this is what awkward looks like—there he was, my dad, in living color. My brain was spanning the globe, trying to find the comfort zone within myself to be okay with this moment. The separate parts of me started to bubble up with so many different emotions. As one part of me said, "This was crap," another part wanted to grab him and hug him and say, "Don't ever leave. I will never be a problem to you. Just stay and be my dad because I need you to want me. I want to be your little girl, and I forgive you for not being there." Oh, but there was yet the side of me bubbling, boiling, seething with disgust, and just downright mad at every single person who had any knowledge of this and neglected to tell me.

How dare they play with my life as if it was a board game? What could God possibly be telling me in this situation? At this moment, I didn't want to hear from Him either because He knew too. The anger had won.

But I sat there, full in my manners of politeness, and with a sincere effort to try to fake a smile, I started crying. It just felt like another slap in the face to me. I asked God, "And this is what you call life? This is unfair. What did I do to deserve this?" But *my dad* reached out and grabbed my hand and said, "Don't cry."

Who was this man touching me, trying to comfort me at this moment when I'm full of rage? I had never felt these feelings before, a bag of mixed emotions, but those were the sweetest words I had ever heard. It wasn't because I needed to hear them in my life. I never even thought of him *my dad*. I just thought I was a kid without one—a dad, that is. It was because he was my dad, the man who made me. And since it never mattered to me before, why start now? But there he was, sitting across from me, comforting me. He stood me up and hugged me, the best hug I ever got from a person I never knew. Now what am I supposed to do? That was the summer right before my nineteenth birthday.

Though biologically I may not have had a father at my disposal, and some things are best left alone, I have been blessed to have my Heavenly Father, always there.

* * * *

And with all things being of God, and if you'll allow me to jump ahead in my story for a second, I decided I needed to try to establish a traditional moment with my dad. Through some odd desire for tradition, I reached out again to this man who seemingly took the claim of father over me. Planning my wedding, I opted for the idea of my father giving me away. It had a large amount of irony to it. It would satisfy the need to see both my parents together for the first time, as well as having him claim me and give me away all at once, a one-stop shop.

The Meeting at the Wedding. It being a moderate wedding, some very special things took place for me, such as my mother making my wedding dress; it was the most beautiful thing she could have done for me. It was a moment in time when we started to rebuild our relationship, and my heart wanted to make her proud of me, so I asked her to make it, and being the seamstress that she is, she took it on.

We had some very special moments, spending weekends together shopping for wedding things. She helped me as much as she could, put it all together, and it was special. We worked through lace options, satin options, sleeve options, length options. I cannot say it enough; she put so much love and heart into it. I felt like a princess. And I did not stop there. I was also in touch with my father. He agreed to give me away, and I was satisfied with that.

I had reconciled in my mind that I could release them both from any self-imposed guilt that they possessed from my birth, which they both had spent so much time defending their own positions. I never could figure that one out. I tried so many times, desperately, to relieve them of this pressure they put on themselves about trying to make me feel somewhat okay about the circumstances of my birth. But honestly and truly, it never bothered me. I wasn't there when they made the decisions about how they got together. I just happened to be the result of it.

But there we were, the first encounter of my true family, together with me for the very first time. It was surreal, and I had set it in motion. And so I prayed as they finally got together, my mom seeing my dad for the first time in as many years of my current age and my dad seeing my mom for the first time after receiving the news of my existence. There we were, together for the very first time in my life. What had I done and blamed God for, and why had He allowed it?

And so this man, my father, was prepared to walk me down the aisle. I was twenty-six years old and had never before felt love from him, even though I was not sure whether it was real or obligational. What welled up in me was emotion that I didn't know what to do with, but whatever it was, it was overwhelming. God had given it, in its perfect place. It felt as if God had allowed all those missing years to happen all at once. Strange, but there was a moment there when my focus was more on being with my father rather than getting married. And there we stood, at the beginning of the aisle, my arm in his, and he asked me if I was ready; and for that very short moment, I said no to myself as if there was another life for me elsewhere. But when I saw my daughter, standing there as my flower girl, being the most beautiful thing I had ever seen, it was clear; I had to give her exactly what I was experiencing right then, a father's love, since I wasn't so sure whether her father would be able to complete that task, hence giving her the same abandonment issues I had to endure. Sadness had reigned over my life for too long. I had to give happiness one last try for her and myself. I did not want her living with a sad mother. I was going to fight for her, as well as for myself, in every way I could.

There I was, standing in the House of the Lord on my way to His altar, prepared to ask Him to bless a union of marriage, which I had not once asked Him for His guidance on. It was infinitely weird how I could have made this decision of marriage and not included the Lord in it, attempting my hand at correcting my life. There were many lives that were going to be affected by this decision, yet once again, I was determined not to let anyone have a say or a word in what I was doing. Hindsight is something, isn't it?

Now don't get me wrong, I don't regret getting married; what I do regret is not seeking God's face before doing it. God allowed it to be so, and so it was. He blessed me so much that day. He had placed it in my parents' hearts to do this thing for me, and I accepted this blessing with both hands. I was holding on to my father as if I could squeeze the last twenty-six years of missing him from my life into those few moments that we shared walking down the aisle. It's almost as if it would be my last time seeing him.

And as it was, I was not the only one involved in this entire scenario. There were others, seen and unseen, and I had to consider their truths as well. So I haven't seen him since. The claiming ended. I sacrificed my relationship with him so others would be happy. *"Do not hide Your face from me; Do not turn Your servant away in anger; You have been my help; Do not leave me nor forsake me, O God of my salvation"* --Psalm 27:9.

With there being no direction or instruction on how to get through life; no correction, punishment, or chastisement; no teaching on dating or marriage, it was but for the grace of God that I went on. *"And you, fathers, do not provoke your children to wrath, but bring them up in the training and admonition of the Lord"* --Ephesians 6:4.

HINDSIGHT @ 20/20

As always, there were questions surrounding what seemed to be natural or unnatural occurrences in my life, but it was always an ending with some supernatural result. I knew God had some part in it. What else could it be? No matter where the event started, by the time the Lord was through with it, I always saw His hand in it, time after time. At this point in my short life, it was the Lord revealing Himself to me in all that I had endeavored to do or whatever crossed my path. My life design developed into lessons and knowledge, securing the fact that I was never alone, that God was always with me.

Somehow I never seemed to pay attention to the signs. I ignored all His showing at every turn. I accepted the presence of God like He was gifting me some special favor as if I was the only one special to Him, not understanding it as grace. I took it sometimes as luck, noting I certainly did nothing to earn this grace and favor from Him. *"But to each one of us grace was given according to the measure of Christ's gift"* --Ephesians 4:7.

What were the lessons learned in my life thus far? Protection, provision, restoration, and reconciliation. God promised me supernatural favor. *"Not by might nor by power, but by My Spirit,' Says the Lord of hosts"* --Zechariah 4:6.

The Lord uncovered a life withheld from me. I may not have had the normal start in life, but I was loved; I may have been unstable in my living, but I was provided shelter without effort on my part; I may have been thrust in the lion's den, but an angel of the Lord protected me from the flames; and I may not have had the father in my life that laid claim over me, but I did have the Father that took possession of me.

Psalm 23
The Lord the Shepherd of His People
A Psalm of David.

The Lord *is* my shepherd;
I shall not want.
He makes me to lie down in green pastures;
He leads me beside the still waters.
He restores my soul;
He leads me in the paths of righteousness
For His name's sake.
Yea, though I walk through the valley of the shadow of death,
I will fear no evil;
For You *are* with me;
Your rod and Your staff, they comfort me.
You prepare a table before me in the presence of my enemies;
You anoint my head with oil;
My cup runs over.
Surely goodness and mercy shall follow me
All the days of my life;
And I will dwell in the house of the Lord
Forever.

TAKING ON LIFE

All about Me. **Now, back to my reality...** Was it time to take the reins for myself? What had the chaos in my life taught me? Had it been the catalyst for me to get to know what I was made of? *"For we are His workmanship, created in Christ Jesus for good works, which God prepared beforehand that we should walk in them"* --Ephesians 2:10. My perspective had shown me a way to see myself through adversity. Not wanting to accept what I was made of, I was forced to see life from a struggling point of view, not a struggling for survival but a struggling for clarity. How focused I became was determined by the way I lived my life. Now I had to refocus myself for my own choices.

I knew the basics of living, but sitting down and planning a directional course of action just wasn't an option for me. My path became the seeing-it-and-picturing-that-it-would-work-for-me option. What I based my growth on was what I thought was done to me when, in fact, it was actually what was provided for me, and that included character through upbringing, integrity through believing in ability, and stick-to-itiveness through determination. It was a view that helped my worldly naïveté, but I can do all things through Christ who strengthens me.

The recent events in my life caused me to grapple with my situation as a whole, with inner urgings forcing my hand. I had contemplated going into the Marine Corps again but wasn't too sure if it was the right thing to do. So it being a Wednesday and raining all day, on my way to the bus stop from work, I asked myself, *What are you going to do here, is this the rest of your life?* Pondering that question on the ride home, I just couldn't stop thinking about it. And in a defeatist attitude, plopping on the sofa still in my wet clothes from the ride home, the feeling of not wanting to be complacent with my life overtook me. Was the Lord urging in His planned direction for my life? *"Have I not commanded you? Be strong and of good courage; do not be afraid, nor be dismayed, for the Lord your God is with you wherever you go"* --Joshua 1:9.

After a few of years of part-time work and attending college for a year, the goal was still ahead of me, but the ability to accomplish it was too great to handle alone; and with not having a place to continue my craft, money running short, limited space available, my options running out, I thought about placing a curious call. Grabbing the phone—I'm not sure whether it was still out of self-disgust or desire, but whatever it was, I let it get the better of me— and being of legal age now, which afforded me the position to look at life without needing permission for my decisions, I placed that call. And what started out as curiosity ended up being my future.

I reached out to the recruiter who I had dealt with the previous year. He wanted to come get me, but I needed constant motion, so I abruptly said, "No, I'll come to you." I jumped back on the trolley, still in the rain, went to the recruiter's office, took care of enlistment paperwork, and caught the trolley home. Yup, I signed the contract. I dropped out of college and enlisted in the United

States Marine Corps. I smiled within myself like a Cheshire cat. It was a proud moment for me for several reasons; I felt I was doing the right thing for myself, and I didn't care what anyone thought of it. It was my decision and my decision alone, *a total preoccupation with myself.*

Now with a profound ability to move ahead, my head was full of selfish aspirations. Finally, with personal authority, I had the audacity to stand up to what used to have such a hold over me. *"Let us lay aside every weight, and the sin which so easily ensnares us, and let us run with endurance the race that is set before us, looking unto Jesus, the author and finisher of our faith, who for the joy that was set before Him endured the cross, despising the shame, and has sat down at the right hand of the throne of God"* --Hebrews 12:1–2. It was clearly another moment of me not being able to assist myself because it was something I had not been able to do before. Who was it that gave me the will and boldness to stand up for myself? It was the He who set my plan in place. *"According to the eternal purpose which He accomplished in Christ Jesus our Lord, in whom we have boldness and access with confidence through faith in Him"* --Ephesians 3:11–12. And so be it, My plan was set, and I had no control except to follow through. Part of me looked at it almost as a would-be failure if I had allowed those powers that questioned me to overrule what was marked as a set path. I was unwilling to live with that.

So as another one of my life's goals was about to empower me further, I set my plans in motion, and the first thing was to not look backward, always onward and forward. The days grew closer to my departure, the looking backward slipped further from my thoughts, and I told myself there was nothing here for me, that my time in this space had ended. ***This is where you never say never.***

And as I stood there to be sworn in and take the oath to defend this country, I was never more proud of myself. The yoke was broken. In my mind, I was free . . . in the land that offered me the very freedom I sought. *"Stand fast therefore in the liberty by which Christ has made us free, and do not be entangled again with a yoke of bondage"* -- Galatians 5:1. So my life began, and all I had to take with me was my hope, my desperation, my desire, and my gratitude; and with all that in tow, I put my life in the hands of the Lord as He put me in the hands of the United States Marine Corps.

On the day of my departure, it was a picturesque morning; looking out at the beautiful big clear blue sky, it felt like my day, a day God had made just for me. My future awaited me. I've been asked so many times, why the Marine Corps? Well, my response is why not the Marine Corps? What was there to be afraid of? Hard work, I had that trying to survive; a sense of pride, I needed that other than what others allowed me to feel. Why diminish what I think my ability is? Why not look to the heavens for direction and guidance for my desires? *"The Lord is my rock and my fortress and my deliverer; My God, my strength, in whom I will trust"* --Psalm 18:2.

Although my start did not afford me the very best out of life, it afforded me mercy, care, and protection, as well as foundational morals and lessons that allowed me to see that I was worth the best, even if others may have treated me like I wasn't. I wanted better than what was handed to me. *"Delight yourself also in the Lord, And He shall give you the desires of your heart"* --Psalm 37:4.

Boot camp was tough, but growing up was even tougher. Trying to navigate through life was infinitely more difficult. This new lifestyle afforded a tearing away of all the non–self-worth and/ or made-up self-worth into what was the definition of a United States Marine. Being among the few who could make it through and standing with the proud, which I became after making it through, I was able to be called a Marine. *Ooh-rah, Marine!*

Life in this new place was altogether rewarding, difficult, pleasing, with a slice of unhealthy. It turned what was already a hard shell into an even harder shell. As the inside of me was constantly begging the Lord to never leave me, a subsequent battled also raged on. Even though I saw myself fearless, my life could not get any worse. *And so I thought.*

I grew into the part; I learned from others a way that allowed me to present myself as if I knew already what to do. I had a few very good friends who came into my life during this time, and I also picked up habits—some good, some not so good. I took a few paths that were against God, all the while dealing with the internal conviction of right and wrong. I hid behind the culture that I was committed to as I gave myself excuses to behave in a manner that was at times totally inappropriate for me, as well as those around me. It was a period of major regret along with sustainable pride.

The duty afforded the opportunity to live off base, and I jumped on it. Yep, it was my first apartment, furnished, but it was mine. It was a one-bedroom that was located on a second-floor catwalk with a bay window, which looked over the Chesapeake Bay. All I saw was sand and water. It was an extremely beautiful view to look at day and night, seeing what God had created. Really, Lord, this is the sight you gave me? Why would God allow this for me? *"In the beginning God created the heavens and the earth"* --Genesis 1:1. Again, I was questioning myself, always living with this innate feeling that I was not worthy of this type of blessing, nor was I supposed to enjoy it. Who has cast this belief upon me? Who has chastened my spirit to believe this was my fate, endeavoring just to survive? Had I allowed it to happen to me, or was I unconsciously under some diabolical Machiavellian scheme to live a life of feeling less than. *"But we are bound to give thanks to God always for you, brethren beloved by the Lord, because God from the beginning chose you for salvation through sanctification by the Spirit and belief in the truth"* --2 Thessalonians 2:13.

But there I was, experiencing this beautiful blessing from God, which he allowed me to experience, a dream and desire of mine, and all I could think of was who did I need to appease in order to receive it. *"And seeing the multitudes, He went up on a mountain, and when He was seated His disciples came to Him. Then He opened His mouth and taught them, saying: 'Blessed are the poor in spirit, For theirs is the kingdom of heaven. Blessed are those who mourn, For they shall be comforted. Blessed are the meek, For they shall inherit the earth. Blessed are those who hunger and thirst for righteousness, For they shall be filled. Blessed are the merciful, For they shall obtain mercy. Blessed are the pure in heart, For they shall see God. Blessed are the peacemakers, For they shall be called sons of God. Blessed are those who are persecuted for righteousness' sake, For theirs is the kingdom of heaven. 'Blessed are you when they revile and persecute you, and say all kinds of evil against you falsely for My sake. Rejoice and be exceedingly glad, for great is your reward in heaven, for so they persecuted the prophets who were before you'"* --Matthew 5:1–12. It was only an apartment with a beautiful view, but I saw it as something where the Lord looked down and said He wanted just me to have.

Still living with my devotion to my past, I couldn't I just walk away from it. It just seemed to haunt me. I couldn't seem to get a hold of the anger that plagued me. Why did I let myself become such an angry person when I saw myself as one who could love with the passion that would complete anyone needing it. *"And do not grieve the Holy Spirit of God, by whom you were sealed for the day of redemption. Let all bitterness, wrath, anger, clamor, and evil speaking be put away from you, with all malice. And be kind to one another, tenderhearted, forgiving one another, even as God in Christ forgave you"* --Ephesians 4:30–32.

Without giving any excuses for my behavior and accepting full accountability for my own actions, I allowed the anger to overtake me. I found myself violating God's laws and plans for my success in ways that had never crossed my mind before. It was my path of self-destruction. I destroyed my own moral code for behavior with wickedness I possessed and exposed others to, my own personal blueprint for my own personal demise. It was the most unhappy I had ever been with myself. It seemed particularly vicious because I knew what I was doing. And this wasn't a viewpoint given to me; it was mine, and I felt out of control. *"Therefore, since Christ suffered for us in the flesh, arm yourselves also with the same mind, for he who has suffered in the flesh has ceased from sin, that he no longer should live the rest of his time in the flesh for the lusts of men, but for the will of God. For we have spent enough of our past lifetime in doing the will of the Gentiles—when we walked in lewdness, lusts, drunkenness, revelries, drinking parties, and abominable idolatries. In regard to these, they think it strange that you do not run with them in the same flood of dissipation, speaking evil of you. They will give an account to Him who is ready to judge the living and the dead. For this reason the gospel was preached also to those who are dead, that they might be judged according to men in the flesh, but live according to God in the spirit"* --1 Peter 4:1–6.

This time, it was a different feeling of not being able to assist in my own survival or the results that were birthed from it. My actions had forced others to live by my decisions just as it was imposed upon me. Was the past a foretelling of my future, not knowing just how damning my actions were to those who were affected by it? I felt horrible.

I felt I was being blessed and cursed at the same time. My whole understanding of who I was and where I was going and what my purpose was totally seemed to take a backseat to my immediate pride, which was at issue. I had to make it right; it became a principal thing. I wound myself up into this self-creation. As I progressed through this period in my life, God was still blessing me, covering me, and protecting me all at the same time; but I wasn't counting my blessings. I was just under the false pretense that I was creating my own reality. My continued self-importance allowed me to think that it was by my hand that I made it out of my bad situation and by my hand that I made it to where I was. The self-righteousness I imposed upon myself, for lack of better words, was lacking all glorious measures. But yes, God had allowed me to continue with this false pretense I possessed because the lesson of humility was on the way. *"The fear of the Lord is the instruction of wisdom, And before honor is humility"* --Proverbs 15:33. So it was within this state of my being that I met a man who would be my husband.

* * * *

Marriage. It turned for me into the experience of a lifetime. As opposites, we attracted each other, and we jumped in head-on.

It was a very short engagement, and we were married within the year. And not at any point did I seek God's face for my decision. *"Glory in His holy name; Let the hearts of those rejoice who seek the Lord! Seek the Lord and His strength; Seek His face evermore! Remember His marvelous works which He has done, His wonders, and the judgments of His mouth"* --Psalm 105:3–5.

This man I married, how could he know what he was getting? How could I know what I was getting? We hardly spent enough time getting to know each other before deciding to undertake the responsibility of marriage. But we had a beautiful wedding, escorted by a 1921 Model T, through the streets of Philadelphia, after being married in my grandmother's church. My family put on a wedding to suit all onlookers. But I was determined to prove the point that I had my husband and my career, and I was pressing on with my life. To my chagrin, what lurked just ahead in this new life I chose was an even a bigger mystery, and I chose it for myself.

We had to deal with this military obligation, getting to know each other, families, and friends, each to their own, and that's how we went about it. Even though I was married, I still lived a very comfortable life of being by myself because my husband was very comfortable living a life filled with his own friends almost as if he was not even married to me. I was determined to "do my own thing." I was going to do what I wanted and when I wanted, somehow still needing to prove a point to my past. But how could he know what lurked beneath my surface? I know I never told him just how pathetic I thought what I had gone through was; I didn't want him to think of me as unworthy. I couldn't take another disappointment in my life, so I jumped in, wholly accepting the fact that he wanted me to be his wife. So I laid all my expectations at his feet, unbeknownst to him. *"For I know the thoughts that I think toward you, says the Lord, thoughts of peace and not of evil, to give you a future and a hope" --Jeremiah 29:11.*

He didn't have a clue that my life was full of the expectations I held; it was unfair to him because I never told him, yet I expected him to know. He thought he was getting a normal woman, full of ambition and stability, when I knew he was getting a broken, damaged creature, full of resentments. I placed every bit of my desperation and perceived life defaults at his feet without his knowledge and then expected him to fix me. And when he didn't fix me, when he set his pace on being himself, I blamed his character. "He wasn't man enough for me" were my sorted words. I knew the life that I lived every day was missing so many pieces.

I began to pour myself into being a wife first, and then second was being a Marine. It was the cost of trying to feel whole. My expectations of him were greater than he could have ever imagined. I laid my life's problems before him and expected him to make me whole and feel like the woman I thought I was on the inside, propel us into heavenly places, and give me the picturesque ever after I demanded; and when he didn't, I, in my heart, discarded him.

As my storybook life raged on, a year and a half later, I was blessed with my beautiful daughter. My head was in a whirlwind. I had never been pregnant before. What was I supposed to do? There was no one I could call or tell. Was I supposed to give up my career for this man and have a baby? *"Then God blessed them, and God said to them, 'Be fruitful and multiply'"* --Genesis 1:28. Just as I was beginning to settle in with this new lifestyle, my husband made life-changing decisions that would affect not only his world but also our world as a married couple with a child.

There was no lonelier time in my life. I learned to count on the disgust I felt for the decisions made, decisions he chose that best suited him, but they were decisions that gave me no choice. I was compelled to make drastic decisions myself, decisions I felt best suited me and the welfare of my child, decisions that I had no support to make, nor did I consider the consequences for making them and for the reasons I made them. It was the reasons that gave rise to my excuses. I didn't even consider where these excuses would take me. The idea was to survive and save face, my face, my own self-humiliation. How could I—me, the smart one, the separate one—find myself living this life? It was my own setup, a pride-filled setup. *"Pride goes before destruction, And a haughty spirit before a fall"* --Proverbs 16:18. Was this the beginning of my downfall? Had I set things in motion for my continued failure? I did not want to spend any time focusing on what it was that was decided for me, but the process of accepting the decision is what mattered. He forced my hand without my input and then expected me to go along with it with no consequence. It was not where I saw my life going, nor was it something I wanted to deal with in my lifetime. I was given an option, and I chose not to accept it. Truth be told, it really could have been almost anything; but if it wasn't a lifestyle I had perceived in my mind as doable or a decision that I was part of, I was not going along with it.

Going along to get along, with saving-face options, I endeavored to not make waves. My life's situation was out of control, and my thought process was out of control. There was nothing I could do to rein any of it in. I had a husband and a child. I was living the dream with the precept that I was doing what God wanted me to do. I had set it up perfectly. I had afforded myself the ability to continue to separate myself from others who were not living according to what God had said. It was a pretense, self-promoting.

It was pride, and this is what it looks like, feels like, and gives you—self-destruction. And I was looking at it through horse blinders but not horse blinders given as a gift from God, not this time.

Time moved on without me. I was clueless what to do next. This festered within me, and it was that festering that developed into a hate for my situation. And being more married to the hate than the man, I lived with it every day. I slept with it, woke with it, ate with it, did all manner of things with this hate that had become my passion. I even began to depend on the hate I felt because it was the only sustaining factor that was constant within me at that moment. *"But he who hates his brother is in darkness and walks in darkness, and does not know where he is going, because the darkness has blinded his eyes"* --1 John 2:11. I struggled with the feelings that I felt, which were forced upon me because of my obligation. There I was, dealing with feelings that I set deep inside my psyche and how my life needed to change because of my choice to marry this man. It was resentment through and through. But who did I resent more, me or him?

And after much sulking, I began to gain a strength that I had not known before. I had to have purpose again, and I did; only this purpose was to protect the one who could not protect herself, my child, and I was going to fight for her with all that I had. And since I've always counted myself as a forward-thinker, I prided myself with preparing for the next step in my life *(false pride rearing its ugly head again because if I was good at it, I would have planned better than I did for this time in my life),* not even considering the fallout from leaving one situation to the next; the most important thing was to make it out of the insufferable situation intact.

So I had to make a decision in which direction I was going to take my life. I had to aid in my own survival as I saw it, even though I was still not seeking God's face. *"The preparations of the heart belong to man, But the answer of the tongue is from the Lord. All the ways of a man are pure in his own eyes, But the Lord weighs the spirits. Commit your works to the Lord, And your thoughts will be established. The Lord has made all for Himself, Yes, even the wicked for the day of doom. Everyone proud in heart is an abomination to the Lord; Though they join forces, none will go unpunished. In mercy and truth Atonement is provided for iniquity; And by the fear of the Lord one departs from evil. When a man's ways please the Lord, He makes even his enemies to be at peace with him. Better is a little with righteousness, Than vast revenues without justice. A man's heart plans his way, But the Lord directs his steps"* --Proverbs 16:1–9.

* * * *

The People Who Cross Your Path. It was at this point that I believe God got tired of laughing at me making a mockery of my life and sent someone across my path. As always, just when you think you've solved your own problems, there's the problem you least expect. It's often a strange thing how you meet people, most often not through your own doing but through circumstances. And it was through a set of circumstances that I met a friend who would become my sister for life. While keeping my feelings internally separate, I wasn't sure just what this all meant, but it was the first time in my life that I had someone I was willing to confide any of my emotions to. It had been a constant for me not to stay in one place and maintain any long-term friendship, but it was a friendship that allowed two women from similar backgrounds to have camaraderie, and it felt like we both held on for dear life.

Now you might ask why this particular story would be important, but oh, yes, it's majorly important. It was through growing in this friendship that I was able to see myself as the woman on the outside, who I had been struggling with on the inside. She was me, and I was her, both angry about the past, maintaining strength in order to keep it hidden, and loving those around us as hard as we could to cover up painful events of the past. It was eerie to see myself outwardly in someone else because I had prided myself with separation. *"A man who has friends must himself be friendly, But there is a friend who sticks closer than a brother"*--Proverbs 18:24. And although I felt compassion for her struggles, I was still unwilling to divulge my innermost painful secrets. Being the best of friends now for some thirty-two years, I still haven't been able to reveal all my past to her; but ever so slowly, I have been able to divulge who I am and what I've been through, and so has she. Although it has been painful to tell mine and hear hers as well, we have begun to let the pain go.

Learning we had been suffering with some of the same issues, we would provide advice to each other as if we could solve each other's dilemmas; but when you're unwilling to deal truthfully with the emotions behind a situation, what you ultimately end up doing is trying to fix the problem that belonged to someone else and, in turn, unsuccessfully fixing yourself.

As life continued on, even though I felt stuck in my situation because of my obligations, I started counting my blessings, and one of them was this new life that I was responsible for. So I did my enlistment and got out.

* * * *

The Birth of a Family. The security of living within yourself often leads to a battlefield of unpreparedness of the world around you. And so I set my life yet in another direction. *"The proverbs of Solomon the son of David, king of Israel: To know wisdom and instruction, To perceive the words of understanding, To receive the instruction of wisdom, Justice, judgment, and equity; To give prudence to the simple, To the young man knowledge and discretion—A wise man will hear and increase learning, And a man of understanding will attain wise counsel, To understand a proverb and an enigma, The words of the wise and their riddles. The fear of the Lord is the beginning of knowledge, But fools despise wisdom and instruction"* --Proverbs 1:1–7. Was this adjusting and readjusting ever going to slow down? It was a perplexing thought. It seemed at every turn, every growth, there was another direction I was headed. What was God doing with me? Where was he sending me?

While I watched others settle within their normalcy, I was in a decision-making position, ready to uproot my life and head somewhere else. Am I repeating the once disgusted life I thought I had? Had my disgust been for nothing, or was that constant moving preparing me for this moving? So when these decisions of mine started to take form, I had my whole plan set out, just what I was going to be doing for the rest of my life. Call it strange, but in my youth, I had decided at one time that I was going to be a career Marine, never get married, and never have children. And by the time I was ready for the Marine Corps, I had spent a good majority of my life by myself, so it was an easy decision to make—solitude, security, and future. What more could an angry, disgusted, and fed-up woman want? It was nirvana. But as God always seemed to have something else planned for my life; here we go again, another one of my life's decision or heavenly directional paths. *"But God draws the mighty away with His power; He rises up, but no man is sure of life. He gives them security, and they rely on it; Yet His eyes are on their ways. They are exalted for a little while, Then they are gone. They are brought low; They are taken out of the way like all others; They dry out like the heads of grain"* --Job 24:22–24.

* * * *

By this time, I had been in touch with my mother more frequently, and we were working on our relationship or the lack there was of it, as well as trying to forge ahead with my life. I left Virginia and returned to Philly. *Here is the never say never part.* Reconciling with my mother was sometimes a bumpy road. Having never addressed with her the pains of my youth, we tugged at this mother-daughter relationship like it was a calling of our life from God, and it turned out to be just that. Although we were not sure how to address it from either side, we stuck it out.

Although I had to suck up my emotional response to my situation, I had to do something or settle for a lifestyle that would compromise my life as well as my daughter's life for someone's madness. So what I did was, after telling my then-husband that it was insane if he thought I would even consider a lifestyle that would jeopardize or harm me and/or my daughter and that I had had enough, I took my two days of clothes and my daughter and left him sitting on the bed—our bed, our marriage bed—and walked out. And he did nothing to try to get me to stay. It was as if—no, not as if but his actions said the words that his mouth didn't: "Accept my selfishness, live this suspect lifestyle, support me in my efforts, allow our daughter to witness and learn from it, and shut up while you're doing all that." Well, since we are playing chess and it was my move, I had to allow my actions to say what he obviously didn't believe my mouth said, which was, in essence, "Sit right there. Don't move. I'll be right back," and so I left him there, sitting on the bed, watching me leave. And with my baby in tow, I rolled out.

Now what? There I went again, but this time, I was not alone.

* * * *

On to the Next. That night was the longest night of my life. My response was definite, and the only place I could go was back to the one place I tried everything in my power to leave, my grandmother's house. My options were limited, and my anger was greater than what my other option left me. I was again feeling this powerful anger, which quickly developed into me revisiting that previous hate position. How quick I was to feel this emotion.

I never saw myself wanting to hate someone. Angry, yes, but hate at this level, I did not know I had it in me, but there it was, this powerful emotion that I seemingly had no control over, or so I thought at that time. Hate was nothing I ever sympathized with or even considered that I'd have to deal with, but I had experienced it several times in my life, questioning if it was really hate or disgust disguised as hate. It had been an emotion that I pretty much used as a euphemism to go along with an angry expletive. But there I was, angrier than I've been, and that was mainly because I had put all my hopes into what I thought would be my life and how it should look and feel, and it was really not even given a chance. The relationship and marriage was very short-lived, and even within that short period, I did not stand up for myself until I was left with no options. He went on with life as if there was no one in his life but him, not leading his family in a Godly direction, nor did he consider the damage all this was causing; and worst of all, I sat there and let him do it. So who was worse, the doer or the enabler? The doer is only going to do for himself, but the enabler allowed the dissension. This behavior I learned from watching myself in my youth, unable to assist in my own defense. I continued to conduct myself in much the same way, so it felt normal as a learned behavior. So I tucked my tail, held my chin up, held on to my daughter for dear life, and walked into my future without him. I was not planning on looking back. It was the birth of my family, without him.

Those choices of his made me feel second class to his dumb ideas, and I did not want to accept that. Did he not know how much I was willing to give of myself to this marriage? Me, that was all I had, and I was willing to devote 110 percent of it to having the family I always wanted. I was not about to be second to anything because I knew that would only be the beginning. The first thing was lifestyle, then family, friends, not working, disrespect, and on and on. I was not, under any circumstance or compromise, going to have someone destroy what I believed to be my fairy-tale life, not by hook or crook. So I just kept the dream alive within me.

I didn't even call my grandmother to tell her I needed to come back, and I was bringing someone with me. I just showed up at the door. I walked in, and there was a family member sitting in the living room, and as they asked me, "What are you doing here?" I had no comeback except to tell my truth, and that was I had just left my husband. Uttering the words from my mouth felt so foul and dirty as if someone had filled my mouth with something unmentionable, as I couldn't even form words to voice my own disdain and disgust for myself, let alone how someone else might view it. Nonetheless, I walked in the door and into the living room, and upon answering the question posed to me, the response was even more surprising; they laughed as if I had told them a joke as they uttered, "That's what you get." I'm still dumbfounded, thinking that someone cared so little of me that my desperate and sad situation would bring humor to them, like a source of entertainment.

So I stood there with my daughter in my arms as I tried to compose myself, all the while asking myself in that split second, *What do I do now? Do I lash out, cuss them out, cry? What?* It was a shaking-my-head moment. Was I coming to the end of myself? This was clearly my first great failure, and I was not handling it well. I wasn't sure how I was supposed to handle it, but I knew I wasn't going to take it lying down. There was no way I was going to let them see me sweat.

So I marched myself upstairs to my grandmother's room, and there she was, sitting on her bed, her sanctuary, and I came in with my daughter in hand, and I just stood there in the doorway and cried. Why I was crying perplexed me even more. Was it because I had purposefully ended my marriage without a second thought? Was it that I felt so disrespected? Was it because I had to return to the one place again where I had told myself I would never come back to? Or maybe it was just all of those, with each reason fighting for dominance.

I remember the gentle caress of my daughter's hands against my face to wipe away my tears. She was nine months old. She saw me crying and grabbed my face with both of her tiny little hands and just held my face and kissed me. It was the sweetest kiss I had ever had. Wow! Here I had this little life that I was responsible for, and she's looking at me because she had no one else to help her understand this life she was brought into, and she didn't know at this moment what I had just done. All she saw was her mommy crying, and she wanted to help me with the only thing God let do at that time, and that was to show me that it was okay, and that she loved me, the sweetest thing that had ever happened to me. Seeing how my daughter loved me through her eyes was beautiful, peaceful, and divine.

But it was my grandmother who, once again, showed me a side of love that I needed more than anything. She said, "Come sit down, and let's figure this out." She asked me what I wanted to do, and the only response I had was that I needed to sleep. I was hungry because I hadn't eaten, and since I had decided that I did not want any money from him because of how he had acquired it, I left empty-handed, with only what money I had saved; so my grandmother made me something to eat. I bathed my daughter and put her to bed. I'm not sure if I was even able to sleep after that. God had to be revealing something here, but what was it? I changed my life with ultimatums and with the determination to have things my way, calling it the right way. This was not for His glory. It was to satisfy my disgust. *"Who among you fears the Lord? Who obeys the voice of His Servant? Who walks in darkness And has no light? Let him trust in the name of the Lord And rely upon his God"* --Isaiah 50:10.

I asked myself, *Why was it so okay for me to just walk away from this marriage?* There have been so many questions and way too many acceptable reasons. The bottom line is I accepted the finality of it way too easy, without a second thought. I didn't fight for it; I just dismissed it, just as he did, and I jumped right into action.

* * * *

So there I was at this very interesting point in my life, as my situation was still increasingly changing. As my life was always in flux, I had been struggling in some areas and having prosperity in others. How was it that my direction was clear in one sense and totally misguided and misdirected in others? What was God telling me, showing me, expecting of me? What had I been ignoring? I had no clue. Did I seek His face with this new chapter in my life? Yes, kinda, sorta. Only in the sense of provision, continued success, and a father for my daughter. I had to fix what was broken.

I had outlined my priorities in life, one by one, and listed them down; the checklist was in order, and I was on full steam ahead. And although things did not pan out like I wanted them to, I was determined to set things back in order, but first, I had to deal with what was sitting in front of me. My girlhood dream was effectively not going to happen as I saw it; now how do I right the wrong? This was where things start to get a little peculiar.

It had been a dream of mine not to raise my children like I was raised—feeling ignored, unloved, with no father, and with no one to turn to. Acknowledging the feelings that I tried my very best to pass off as survivor skills was an act that I could have won an Academy Award for, but deep inside, I was an extremely sad person. I just couldn't have things my way. I cried continuously, but I rarely let anyone see that side of me, the side that would allow them to see my pain exposed. I didn't need their comments, their way of looking at things, advice, smart remarks, or pity. It wasn't going to change my situation from what it was. I had to change it. And although I did believe in Jesus, I thought it was my responsibility to get off my butt and make things happen for me, and that He would bless those endeavors.

So there, that was the answer. Just keep working toward putting my life together as I saw it and particularly not caring about what anyone thought or said or did, just so I could somehow get to where I thought God wanted it to be—living right. *"I know how to be abased, and I know how to abound. Everywhere and in all things I have learned both to be full and to be hungry, both to abound and to suffer need. I can do all things through Christ who strengthens me"* --Philippians 4:12–13. *And* still being blessed, my position within this company I was working for grew tremendously. Now all my decisions where self-serving for my current situation, and that situation was my daughter's emotional upbringing. I could not allow her to experience what I had growing up.

* * * *

Not the Same as Before. And after a bit of time and my divorce finalized, I started dating a man I met at work, which turned out to be a very freeing relationship for me. The relationship grew quickly. My daughter was still young and barely had seen her father. She started displaying the pains of not seeing him, and I was determined to love her for the both of us. Why would I go right into another relationship for the sake of emotional maintenance and repair?

And although my intention was to set things right before the Lord, there was still great apprehension about who to have in her life. The things I saw in him were genuine, loving, caring. I was going to do things different this time, while still having to deal with my moral issues. We had talked about a future together, and we even displayed playing house together, but was this truly where I saw myself? My internal struggles of not wanting to give my daughter the life I had and being morally judged as what I thought I knew to be right and true and correct in the eyes of God weighed the most within my soul. I felt it tugging at me ever-presently. What was I supposed to do? What choice was I supposed to make at this stage of my life? *"Trust in the Lord with all your* heart, *And lean not on your own understanding; In all your ways acknowledge Him, And He shall direct your paths"* --Proverbs 3:5–6. Now at this point, I had gained some experience with people, places, and wrong choices, using all the faith in myself that I should have displayed in God. I stepped into this new life, and I brought my daughter into it as well. Because I was still living with the rage I had been feeling, I had truly abandoned all hope for success. I was dealing with multiple personality efforts, putting forth love, hate, sorrow, and guilt, with the need to succeed all at the same time. Had I mastered the art of categorizing my emotional states? They all seemed like they were under light switch control. I would turn them off and on as I walked in the room that needed them. And I was the master of it all.

The biggest problem before me was presentation, how I presented myself before my world. Believing presentation was everything, I could not let the world in to my hot mess of a life, so my disguise increased and continued. *"He who hates, disguises it with his lips, And lays up deceit within himself"* --Proverbs 26:24. No one knew as long as I maintained my inward discrete. I had to manage it all, and this is where denial came into play. And so as I speak of denial, I reference only the denial of seeking out God's face on what He wanted for me versus the plan I had. All I needed to do was to execute it. I set myself in motion, praying for all the things I needed to make it all right with God. So with that in play, we decided to move in together. My daughter was happy, my man was happy, and I was happy.

But things weren't always what they were set up to be, and sometimes we purposefully ignored the warning signals because we were determined to have things our way. We lived four almost, *almost* blissfully happy years together in my home state, but as with all things, change would come. Oftentimes, I thought, **What could God be thinking of my actions?** There I was claiming to be a child of God, a follower of Jesus Christ, a true believer in the Gospel of Jesus Christ, yet I was living in a constantly transitional life. I acted as if my micromanaging skills were exact and precise, while I was still broken. I had never healed from my childhood; I took on the Marine Corps, being away from home without any family for the first time; I took on getting married without truly knowing who I was marrying or allowing him to know who he was truly marrying; I took on a job that clearly required a level of devotion from me that I couldn't give; and now I was taking on another relationship without healing from any prior one. And the winner for the best actress was . . . me. Thank you for my award.

My professional world had changed. It moved me to Maryland. There was no reason to stay in Philly, and with so much change happening in my life at that time, I could only remember what my grandmother used to tell me when I was younger. "When you have a lot of confusion, there's always change." I remembered that as if it was my mantra for focus and direction, always looking for the change that was to come out of this whirlwind of confusion. But we went ahead and made the changes professionally and personally.

We moved and were prepared to take on the world. A new home, new positions, a new marriage, a new extended family, a new geographic location, a new church, new friends, and a new trust for one another. Things were moving so fast I really didn't have time to evaluate where I was headed with my personal life; it just felt right. I was so very happy. My happily ever after was happening, and all I could do was ask myself why would God give me a second chance at happiness. I didn't stop to think whether it was something I really should be doing. All I knew was that I was putting my life in order for God's approval. It felt good to be rectifying the mistakes I had made jumping into a marriage without consulting God or anyone else. I just had to make it right for my daughter's sake. She was so precious to me, and she was mine; no one could take her away.

* * * *

There was a kind of peace that had overtaken the far-reaching vision for myself. I almost felt that I had not been lying to myself about ever wanting to be married. The battle I was having with myself always included God. Not that I could ever know what it was like for Jacob to wrestle with God, but it sure felt like I was tackling what I thought God wanted from me and what direction I was actually supposed to be taking. *"For what I am doing, I do not understand. For what I will to do, that I do not practice; but what I hate, that I do. If, then, I do what I will not to do, I agree with the law that it is good. But now, it is no longer I who do it, but sin that dwells in me. For I know that in me (that is, in my flesh) nothing good dwells; for to will is present with me, but how to perform what is good I do not find. For the good that I will to do, I do not do; but the evil I will not to do, that I practice. Now if I do what I will not to do, it is no longer I who do it, but sin that dwells in me"* --Romans 7:15–20.

I had made my mind up that I was going to do what I thought was what the Lord wanted of me—marriage, children, love, and commitment to Him. I was going to force it, the correctness of it, whether I wanted it or not. I was going to make God proud of me. It all made sense to me that that was what His plan was for me, despite what some subpart of me wanted or desired—career, profession, single life, drama-free, just living as peaceful of a life as possible, not living under the auspices to please others. But that was just what I was doing. It was always an exhausting feeling to try to satisfy some preconceived divine quota. And so I allowed the weirdness of it continue to reign over my life. It actually was a little sick to me to lose against myself and at the same time win against myself. What sick, twisted way of logic I had concocted in my brain to survive. But whatever it was, it had become a baseline as well as a bar for me.

And so I settled into this new life I had created, hoping and praying that God was with me in this madness. I let the chips fall where they may. We began our life as husband and wife. And although we had lived together for a few years before we were married, it was the newness of the placement of positions. It all counted, and it felt appropriate. I finally had given my daughter what my original plan was, a family with both a father and a mother. And we were happy, extremely happy . . . for a while. And as with all situations, outsiders begin to creep in.

It's not always outsiders who are strangers, but most often, it's outsiders who are outside of your marriage but inside of your life. And although they come to your wedding and witnessed your union, with no objection said during the ceremony, they seemed to always find a way to object after you're wed. So this was when it started to get a little complicated. Although we had spent a considerable amount of time in the City of Brotherly Love before moving to another state, we were not married, and outside influences were still there, with outward objections but not objectionable enough to halt what we wanted or needed, and that was to be together. So we pressed on. It was about making our family the way we wanted it and putting aside what all others thought or felt. *Or at least that's what we thought.*

So the part of our vow that stated, "What God has put together let no man put asunder," has often perplexed my understanding of it. "No man," as is stated, would lead me to believe that any outside forces that were not in the inner sanctum of my union were prohibited from participating in it, which would make my union strong and impregnable. And I did believe that in my head. But had I solidified that with my then-husband? Was it really marked in stone, or had I been so needy for filling a void that I was willing to accept, consciously or subconsciously, the meaning that surrounded a situation without first considering the remnants and residue of those closely affected, meaning outside sources? *"Therefore a man shall leave his father and mother and be joined to his wife, and they shall become one flesh"* --Genesis 2:24.

All those people associated with us professionally, personally, or by blood, as if it were synchronized clockwork, all started jockeying for position. We came upon opposition unlike anything I was prepared for. The forces at hand had other desires, and they were determined to not let this become a happily ever after for anyone. As opinions were expressed and positions determined, it began the test of wills.

Looking back on what headspace I was in at that time makes me wonder how I kept it all together. If they gave out awards for performance in real-time living, I certainly should have gotten the best actress award, again living this life that had so many branches on it. I had extended myself to a level that I had no choice but to depend on the Lord and where he was giving me strength to even get up in the morning.

And speaking for the both of us, we jumped in, or at least (speaking for me) I jumped in, with both feet, which was something

I had been known to do—give it my all. I saw myself as a good wife and a good mother, wanting to do all what I perceived God would want of me—give all of myself to my family, make my husband happy, and guide my child to right living. Such wild imaginations eventually took their toll on my self-esteem when I started to witness other things taking the place and having weight in my stead. It was something that kick-started, again, some self-protection within me. And these were things that were needed for life, such as work, church, family, and friends--all the things that challenged my every day but the necessities that required my attention. I refused to believe that we weren't meant to be married because I was blessed with my wonderful son from that marriage, but I do believe that the way it was handled was indicative of how it started out.

I was beginning to lose myself within my daily struggles. I couldn't seem to hold on to the thing that mattered the most to me, loyalty. The forces were stronger than I was, they were more demanding than I was, and they pursued my family with a quiet vengeance, presenting a false sense of necessity. I did not know how to fight things that were needed for us to survive. *"For though we walk in the flesh, we do not war according to the flesh. For the weapons of our warfare are not carnal but mighty in God for pulling down strongholds"* --2 Corinthians 10:3–4. I could not dissuade the manipulation of others, nor could I counter any preconceived idealism from presenting itself and requiring my attention as well. We had to work, my daughter had school and friendships, and we needed to attend church and participate within that.

So why, after eighteen years, were things falling apart right before my eyes? I mean, we began to disagree about everything that remotely seemed like it needed a disagreement. And some of the things that we disagreed on were self-induced on either his part or my part, and we began to torture ourselves with this way of thinking, believing it was most likely the only way to get a foothold on the position we held. I would sit and look at my life and wonder why I was so miserable if my life was so wonderful, pretending that I was living within the happiness we had created. It was an exhausting existence with responsibility tied to it. I was so tired, but if you asked me my truth at that time, I couldn't tell you what I was truly tired of.

So life proceeded as it was supposed to. With promotions from my job, professionally, my world had taken off. I had started college again for court reporting, and I was the financial secretary at our church. I almost couldn't believe that I, the little girl who didn't have a stable home and who felt that no one loved her, had just that—family, job and, friends—but there was still a void.

WORK, WORK, AND MORE WORK

Most assuredly, I say to you, he who believes in Me, the works that I do he will do also; and greater works than these he will do, because I go to My Father. And whatever you ask in My name, that I will do, that the Father may be glorified in the Son. If you ask anything in My name, I will do it.
—John 14:12–14

Work as a disciple of Christ starts with acceptance of Him as your Savior and picking up your cross to follow him. *"When they saw Him, they worshiped Him; but some doubted. And Jesus came and spoke to them, saying, 'All authority has been given to Me in heaven and on earth. Go therefore and make disciples of all the nations, baptizing them in the name of the Father and of the Son and of the Holy Spirit, teaching them to observe all things that I have commanded you; and lo, I am with you always, even to the end of the age.' Amen"* --Matthew 28:17–20.

"Remembering without ceasing your work of faith, labor of love, and patience of hope in our Lord Jesus Christ in the sight of our God and Father"
--1 Thessalonians 1:3

How do we affect one another?

Kingdom Work Never Being Done. While there is living and working every day void of the Holy Spirit, there is certainly living and learning amid the Holy Spirit. They are two distinctively different patterns of existence, and I have done both. It is the experiences from my life that have prompted my behavior, attitude, and responses to people I came in contact with. Just how was I supposed to conduct myself in a world that offered temptation that was sometimes hard to ignore, attitudes that required a defense mechanism in order to maintain, and self-protection in order to survive?

Many of us can expound on the wonders of our achievements, but there are none so glorious except done by the grace of God with the Holy Spirit imparted unto you. *"These things I have spoken to you while being present with you. But the Helper, the Holy Spirit, whom the Father will send in My name, He will teach you all things, and bring to your remembrance all things that I said to you"* --John 14: 25–26.

Life affords us time of great triumphs and, sometimes, even greater loss. With worldly views and acceptance directing us to tell ourselves, "It doesn't matter how you start, only how you finish," or "It's not that you fail but how you deal with the failure," it puts every bit of reaction and correction on ourselves. *"But someone will say, 'You have faith, and I have works.' Show me your faith without your works, and I will show you my faith by my works"* --James 2:18. It leaves out the courage that it takes to seek God's help and direction, through the Holy Spirit, for meaningful results, which keep us focused on pleasing God with our everyday deportment. *"Be of good courage, And He shall strengthen your heart, All you who hope in the Lord"* --Psalm 31:24.

I could list a myriad of blessings that God has bestowed upon me professionally. My professional achievements are *many*, more than I, in my lifetime of working, ever envisioned myself being part of. The Lord has blessed me to be a part of pretty impressive organizations, as well as by being in the company of some pretty amazing people in this season of my work history. I can, of course, sit and name-drop like the best of them. But the one name I've come to drop now more than anything is my Lord and Savior, Jesus Christ. What Jesus did for me when He went to the cross has afforded me to live this life now, seeing the beauty instead of the "why me" or "why not me" syndrome. He took away my desperation and gave me acceptance. I now look at working with the "lead me, guide me, along my way" perspective, and that's only because of God's lovingkindnesses. First He sent His Son for salvation and instruction, and then He sent His Holy Spirit for guidance and support, imparting upon us ways for loving conduct, patience, along with the ability to spread the Gospel of Jesus Christ.

I have encountered many personalities throughout my work life, and it taught me one thing—a judgmental attitude, judging everyone's worth to me. I often said to myself, *Don't let me end up like that*, whatever "that" was. I focused in, once again, on the appropriateness of behavior, only this time it was within the workplace. Now whether it had a nice suit on or an even nicer dress, there wasn't much difference in the proportion of delivery, except to say that it was still the same—ill-intended and self-serving posturing.

The military taught me structure that I did not have, along with a sense of commitment that I needed. I was engaged with fellow Marines who simply loved being that—Marines. "Semper fi." I saw personalities that were true to a cause and united for a common goal but individual in understanding. I saw the willingness to lessen oneself for the pride of the Corps. "Esprit de corps."

Why and how could I have that lessening for an organization or people and not have it for the Lord?

Despite many lessons of military life, I found myself always trying to make it work out for me. Doing what I was told when I was told was the easy part. It was the times when I was left to my own devices that I created more problems for myself, more than anything else, always making sure I stayed within the rules and regulations. It was my own core responsibilities that I had the problem with. As for me, myself, and I, we lived conveniently within the culture, only effectuating opinions and behaviors that kept me safely hidden from total exposure. I lived with my idealism of how I saw things. I really never cared what others thought of me until I was chosen to do a task that would make me a first.

Did I see others looking at me from the standpoint of just joining the Marine Corps, or was it so self-promoting that I didn't care what behaviors I displayed to my fellow Marines or, for that matter, anyone else who was looking? Was my workmanship important to me, or did I trivialize its importance for the sake of pride? *"For we are His workmanship, created in Christ Jesus for good works, which God prepared beforehand that we should walk in them"* --Ephesians 2:10.

I took what I had learned through military life and transferred that thinking and discipline into the civilian world, totally and foolishly expecting others to have some sort of behavioral decorum.

What was I thinking? But that's not to say that I did not come across some very ethical people; I knew and worked with quite a few. I have had some extremely respectable mentors in my life. I felt particularly blessed in that arena. God had blessed me at every turn in my professional development with a mentor or sometimes even a few, who clearly were sent by Him, imparting unto me their prowess for teaching how business worked from very different perspectives, and afforded a learning experience that would rival any perceived thought or dream.

Being awarded a position with an engineering firm, whose primary business was the environment, was something I never thought I would do; nevertheless, I looked forward to being involved with it. It started off as a very simple position, a temporary clerk, which I was happy to have, and within three years, I had been promoted into a position where I was traveling, hiring and firing, attending meetings with executives, going to retreats, starting up and closing down multimillion-dollar projects, and the list goes on. It goes to show that when God blesses, He really does run your cup over. I had experiences with people who were at their professional peak, and I learned from them, and they were willing and eager to teach. That clerk position ended up being the regional accounting coordinator, assistant to a vice president who handled multiple regions, ranging at times up to twenty-three states. God had placed His hands firmly in my career and allowed me to experience ten years with that company. But let's not get too comfortable because there were more lessons ahead. And before the Lord closes one door, He always opens another; we just don't often know it's already been opened. Sometimes we're not sure how long we have to stand in the doorway threshold, between walking out and walking in, but that's where faith comes in.

I ended up being the product of a buyout—a new company, a new way of doing business, no middle man. They wiped an entire regional level out with the stroke of a pen. It's something the Lord had been preparing me for, although I didn't even know he was preparing me for it.

My plate was so full during those years. I'm not even sure how I was able to accomplish it all. As the Lord always demonstrates, when your cup runs over by Him, it looks miraculous. Professionally, I had peaked with this company at the top of the regional level, and the only place left was corporate. I had done a good bit of traveling. I had a nine-year-old daughter and a two-year-old son. We were building a house from the ground up and renting a crazy woman's house while waiting for our house to be finished while living half a block from in-laws (a story unto itself). I was the financial secretary at my church with an additional separate set of problems. I was ending one job while still in school, which was a private college fifty-six miles one way, for a major in court reporting, nonetheless. Oh, and let me not forget, I had a husband too. So where was I in all of that? Once again nestled in the arms of God. *"Even to your old age, I am He, And even to gray hairs I will carry you! I have made, and I will bear; Even I will carry, and will deliver you"* --Isaiah 46:4. There is no way, within my own power, that I would have been able to accomplish all of that without Him. He gave me strength, power, and the energy to do it all. And I did it successfully as long as He was involved. But when I stuck my hand in it, that's when it went kaput.

There are always lessons being taught to us. Do we see them, or are we ignoring them purposefully?

* * * *

When the Church Calls. It wasn't that I did not want to work in the church, but from where I was in my professional life, as well as my homelife, along with going to school, I felt I had no more time for anything else. How could I bear it? *"I am the vine, you are the branches. He who abides in Me, and I in him, bears much fruit; for without Me you can do nothing"* John 15:5.

Having always seen the hand of God work in my life professionally from the time I first started working at age thirteen, it began a surety within me that I could have a future for myself without being dependent of others for my survival. But I was kidding myself; I did need people. I wasn't an island. I wasn't in the world alone, but what I did feel was the need not to depend. I didn't even depend on God, although I knew He was there. I was determined to prove my point, if to no one, then to myself. This was in no way displaying work for the Kingdom. It was totally self-serving.

God was pulling me to Him, and I felt His draw. My daily walk was always pointed in His direction, although I wasn't seeing it as that. It was an inner consuming desire to do all he laid out before me with gratitude and thanksgiving. I welcomed all the challenges before I even knew what they were or why they were there or even before I had a clue what they would yield. It was an inward feeling of invincibility. As long as I felt He was there, superficially accepting His presence, I thought I could complete the task. But let's remember, I oftentimes took the position that it was by my hand that it was accomplished, tough words for someone who struggled with depression. My battle with myself took such a strong hold over me, and the fight for who was going to win was left up to the Lord. I was losing myself within myself. I did not have the strength to fight myself, as I was quickly losing battles even when combating others. I was sinking deeper and deeper into my self-made hole. Without looking for help from God because of my self-inflicted unworthiness, I didn't believe I would receive the help I so desperately needed. My shame had won, as my emotional loss was too great, so I tucked my tail and ran.

* * * *

Doing Church Business. The Lord has always kept my life in constant motion. I would always multitask. There was always something to do. Working in and for a church wasn't what I had on my agenda, but when you desire a total submission unto God, your choice of what to do and when to do turns into Him directing your path and you following. In that path is always work for the Kingdom because Kingdom work *is* never done, but the more excellent thing is to listen to Jesus.

Wondering what more I can take on while symptomatically asking myself what was I thinking adding on to an already full plate, I started working in the church as the financial secretary. There just aren't words that can describe this lesson. I admit I was not truly prepared for what cynicism I had to deal with, working with people who are dealing with a cultured way of life. I had one true goal, and that was to do all I could do—under the unction of the Holy Spirit—to properly manage the position I was tasked with. The resistance from others came from propriety and ownership, which cast an extended shadow over what some saw as rights because of seniority for some level of self-protection. It was here that I began to see that all who worked for God did not necessarily have the belief in the responsibilities for their position.

It wasn't always about how to spend God's money, but it had everything to do with personalities and the willingness to serve according to what the Word said. I see my part as an unwilling participant, which gave me separation and the unwillingness to be held accountable for what I perceived as wrongdoings. I guess my strictness for accountability introduced me as one who was not willing to get along, and that put me on the defensive with many who had been used to ways that I deemed as not Christ-centered.

It was rewarding to be a part of the work involved in putting an addition to an existing edifice, as it was my privilege to be able to participate in the development and construction of it. The countless hours of work from an administrative standpoint brought with it all the lessons of my work history. It was what God had trained and prepared me to do, work for the Kingdom, and for His glory. But I was not prepared for those whom I was surrounded by. I was spiritually unprepared and ill-equipped to handle the many personalities that I had given credence to just because we were in church. I had done no study of God enough to call on Him to intervene. I hadn't even read the Bible enough to combat what I was up against. I was only there, dare I say, because it was the church I had gotten married in, as well as the church of my husband's family. It started with my loyalty to my husband, still connecting my chain links in order to complete my family's outward picture. It was what I thought I had to do as a wife—follow my husband in Christ. Why was I going to argue? We were in church as a family.

But we must be mindful of what we do in the name of God. It was a rough position to be in, and with an already overwhelming load, it was the last thing I needed to do or even add on to my life. But I did, and I gave it my all. Or so I thought. Were it not for the unbelievable personality conflicts brought on by loyalties, I felt I may have stayed in the position for as long as the Lord had wanted me to. But it really wasn't my call, was it? It turned into the lessons of learning to hear God's voice, though I did not perceive it as that.

With disconcerting disagreements between longtime servants, their way of thinking, and my unwillingness to concede to the old ways of doing things, it turned into an action far-reaching anything that resembled God. It forced out of me anger and resentment toward other members in the body because of their willingness to promote outside affiliations in their pursuit to gain a foothold. As I saw it, it was a means to include what was not of God in God's house. And I quickly took offense to it. I stood then, and I'll stand now, as Jesus said in Matthew 21:13, *"And He said to them, 'It is written, "My house shall be called a house of prayer."'"* I was offended and angry and protective, probably more than I should have been, but I did not want to be counted among those who would abuse the responsibility given us by the Lord.

After seven years of serving in the position and then quitting and within that same year was asked to come back for a variety of reasons, I returned with the condition that I would not be staying and that they should be looking diligently to replace me within three months; but that turned into another year yet with the same issues still existing, or was it God who wanted me back? At that time, I could not figure it all out. So I did the job. And when things did not change, I was hurt too much from the discord associated with the position, so I left the church for good. I said I was never going to return. I was done with church and its people. So I left mad.

How could God's people treat me in such a way when all I wanted to do was help, when it was them that asked for me twice? I felt used, abused, physically threatened, mistreated, disrespected, talked about, and unwelcome. It was disgraceful from where I stood. There were things that I witnessed from my time with this place that I would not have wished on my worst enemy. A place where you are supposed to come and bring it to the Lord and worship Him, it was anything but that. I was embarrassed before the membership, God, and my family because of the conduct displayed by all involved. It felt like a weekly war zone; what was I going to be up against next? I couldn't figure out why God wanted me to do this job, outside of the obvious way they had been doing things, and I did have the skill set to help. Why did he want me to work in such conditions? He knew what I was up against with my personal life. Why the add-on, Lord?

I was angry at why I was subjected to the behavior. Did they not know that people were looking at us and judging us on our own behavior? I was determined not to deal with church again, if that's what I was going to get. I'll just do it at home, so that's what I did; I went home to "bedside baptist," and I didn't even really do that, vowing to never go to or work in a church again. It was a painful period. *"And let us consider one another in order to stir up love and good works, not forsaking the assembling of ourselves together, as is the manner of some, but exhorting one another, and so much the more as you see the Day approaching"* --Hebrews 10:24–25. If there was ever a time that I needed the Lord in my life for understanding my sorrow, it was then. But I pressed on.

As always, as it was, right in time, the Lord moved me out of the position because it was soon after that that my life took a turn physically, which I was clearly not prepared for. When you don't have health and strength, no matter what you're capable of doing, there is nothing left of yourself to complete the task.

So being in church was not new to me, but working in one surely was. Not to talk out of school, I was just not used to the archaic environment and attitudes. Or was I the archaic one, with my lack of understanding, lack of patience, lack of love for the body of Christ, and/or my lack of going through it with the Holy Spirit? Was I upset because I couldn't have things my way? *"Create in me a clean heart, O God, And renew a steadfast spirit within me. Do not cast me away from Your presence, And do not take Your Holy Spirit from me. Restore to me the joy of Your salvation, And uphold me by Your generous Spirit"* --Psalm 51:10–12.

* * * *

Working for the Lord Today. Since conceding my obedience to my Father and giving up my own selfish way of looking at things, I was blessed to have my eyes opened to God's presence through His lovingkindness by allowing me to repeat experiences in my life, only this time, the Holy Spirit is with me. *"For the Holy Spirit will teach you in that very hour what you ought to say"* --Luke 12:12.

* * * *

Although my journey to the field of court reporting was perilous, by way of subject matter, distance, agreement, subjugation, and responsibility, I managed through it. I told myself as my own personal mantra, *How bad do you want it?* It was a desire for me, bad enough to endure my own humbling for a field that was something I could not control. I didn't have the knowledge walking in the door, nor did I believe in myself enough to take on such a complicated endeavor. I was forced to ask God for help and then believe that he would help me accomplish the immeasurable task. I was without a choice if I was to go through with it.

The experience of school along with the experience of working, I thought, would be enough to satisfy my cravings, but it still wasn't enough. The desire was insatiable. My hunger for whatever was missing in my life overwhelmed me. I felt as if I was supposed to be doing something else, but I couldn't wrap my mind around what it was. I found myself almost with a dismissive attitude about cases I was listening to. But the Lord, hearing my cries, began to deal with me, and I started attending church *again*, only this time it was to learn what my responsibilities were as a child of the Almighty King. I found myself extremely more empathetic and/ or sympathetic to the plight of others.

I remain reluctantly unwilling to describe any particular case, but suffice it to say, listening to the struggles of those sitting before me, I began to enlist sensibilities within myself to have more compassion for either those who were anxiously and openly looking and asking for the Lord's intervention or those who were so lost to His help that the mere mention of the Lord prompted the disgusted phase of their expression.

Many times, either in my church's Bible study or Sunday school, there have been discussions on how we conduct ourselves when we are in the company of those who are looking down at Christians and what our responses would be to such situations. *"Therefore, brethren, stand fast and hold the traditions which you were taught, whether by word or our epistle"* --2 Thessalonians 2:15. Being in a field where I should have no opinion about either side, it's subjectively more complex to remain impartial and unattached when people are struck by misfortune. Not being the one responsible for making the determination of correctness of who's right and/or who's wrong, my subjectivity value only lies with the record that I'm tasked with taking and keeping. But if the Lord opens the door for discussion about Him, I will follow where He leads.

Although many times my heart has felt sorrow for some who has given testimony before me, regardless of what is at issue, it is with a solemn heart that I am able to silently say a prayer for ease and comfort. I have been witness to hearing some horrific moments through what God has equipped me to do, and I do not take it lightly. My conduct, both professionally and personally, require a level understanding from that of me being a child of God. Both have their responses, but first and foremost, I am responsible to the Lord. Our duty and demeanor has an effect on all those around us. It is through fervent prayer that the Lord is in the midst and that all things work to His Glory.

* * * *

HINDSIGHT @ 40/40

As I was making my way through this life of mine, I was picking up some pretty significant habits—some great, some not so great, some useful, some not so useful—nevertheless, I was able to start my life on my own terms. Some of the understandings and philosophies I had come in contact with either made me angry or made me end up trying to figure out their madness. Waste of my time.

Always taking the stand that this is my life, and I do what I want when I want, and clearly not seeking or listening to the Lord, I allowed myself to be used by others, all the while assuming I had control over what I was doing. It was another insurmountable process to believe for myself and my ability to perpetrate a strong willingness of self, at the same time living as one who compromised her values in order to be accepted. My ability to compromise was something I was unwilling to do among people I could not understand, while accepting the compromise within myself in order to please people I honored, just to be accepted and have my status as being one of them. Talk about a twisted fate.

I was aware and lived according to man's ways, but what I was missing was God's ways, the understanding of it, and the applying of it in my everyday living. Having faith without works is dead, and having works with little to no faith is even deader.

God continually gave me mercies, which I ignored. I had rights and privileges that I took advantage of. I had spent so much of my life trying to tweak together the perfect existence, all the while losing myself deeper down the rabbit hole of despair. Life was handed to me as a gift from God, and the only thing I had learned was how to squander it. Oh, the useful parts were useful, but the meaningful parts only benefited me.

After a childhood of others inflicting emotional pain upon me, I then took the gauntlet and continued emotionally abusing myself. Making choices for personal gain was fruitless. I had personally planned a picture in my head and tried to fit others into it. Putting my idealism first and playing second-class citizen to my own value turned into depression. Not having my way felt impossible, but the lessons learned through the hardships is what caught my attention. I ignored my pain as if it really wasn't there. I felt the farthest from God than I had ever been.

I was unprepared for living life, I was unprepared for life's challenges, I was unprepared to stand up for myself, I was unprepared to help others. I've always defined success for myself as preparation meeting opportunity, and I needed just that, preparation, because I had been failing. And it was through my misfortune of having to start all over, being alone and cornered within myself, that my prayers were answered.

* * * *

The Whole Armor of God

Finally, my brethren, be strong in the Lord and in the power of His might. Put on the whole armor of God, that you may be able to stand against the wiles of the devil. For we do not wrestle against flesh and blood, but against principalities, against powers, against the rulers of the darkness of this age, against spiritual *hosts* of wickedness in the heavenly *places*. Therefore take up the whole armor of God, that you may be able to withstand in the evil day, and having done all, to stand.

Stand therefore, having girded your waist with truth, having put on the breastplate of righteousness, and having shod your feet with the preparation of the gospel of peace; above all, taking the shield of faith with which you will be able to quench all the fiery darts of the wicked one. And take the helmet of salvation, and the sword of the Spirit, which is the word of God; praying always with all prayer and supplication in the Spirit, being watchful to this end with all perseverance and supplication for all the saints.

--Ephesians 6:10–18

THE PROCESS OF HEALING

Now it is the blood of Jesus that cleanses us from all unrighteousness, and it is that cleansing that was needed to get me through one of the toughest seasons to date, my demise. I had manifested my desires into real anguish. It was the process of working my lifelong ambitions into what was tangible living, fitting everything and everyone into the mold I had created for my path. All they had to do was just follow my lead.

Also, there began to be too many unsatisfied portions of my life, and that led to too many unanswered questions. There was a tug-of-war, a pull of sorts, between what I saw for myself and an unmarked path set before me; at least it was unmarked by me, a sort of unknown goal or destination, pulling me and urging me in a direction I was unsure of. I just couldn't figure it out. Why weren't things working the way I had planned them? I had laid all the groundwork, I had done all my due diligence, I had even done a few additional things to bolster the engagement of my plans, but there was only one problem. I wasn't exactly sure how to get things set in stone for my own satisfaction. I was losing the battle piece by piece.

I had wrestled with my inner self, I had wrestled with my marriage, I had wrestled with my church, I had wrestled with other family members and friends, I had wrestled with sinful acts, and I had wrestled with my disobedience to God. It was more than my heart, my soul, or my mind could bear. I needed a whole healing, an inner peace, and I needed it now. Jesus had to work things out for me. I could do it no longer.

I was also living with physical disturbances to my health, which had taken a toll on my well-being, which required surgery to save my life, and that became the catalyst for a change that had to come. I could no longer live with the angst of where I found myself. So why was there this additional pull to mentally, emotionally, and spiritually be somewhere else? Why was there this constant self-interrogation of my direction? *"For though we walk in the flesh, we do not war according to the flesh. For the weapons of our warfare are not carnal but mighty in God for pulling down strongholds, casting down arguments and every high thing that exalts itself against the knowledge of God, bringing every thought into captivity to the obedience of Christ"* --2 Corinthians 10:3–5.

Through it all, I still carried its weight every day all day, as it was a second job, making sure the weight had been given enough attention or else I would be punished, or at least I would punish myself even more. I woke up with it every morning, and it was the first thing I thought of. It was my crutch. I couldn't get along without it. It had caused such a depression in me that I started to act out, just to save my own face within myself. I couldn't feel like a failure. I could not lose my life's work of myself to myself. There became such a separation in my relationships that I saw no way for repair, giving me rationale and license to believe that the reasoning I told myself would make it good enough for an exit strategy from any relationship. Had I had enough? I felt like I was exercising my rights of tolerance, but I was tired of the fight. It was enough. I had seen the mean-spirited intentions toward me for the last time, even coming from me. I was not willing to tolerate it any further. I was ready to strike out.

I found myself in physical pain behind it. I was so unhappy that I did not know what I was more unhappy about—their actions or me tolerating their actions. It felt like a lifetime, and I did not want to spend another moment of my life dealing with it any further. I had to save my face, my dignity. I could not let them win over me. I felt destroyed. I had loved so hard and given my all so that there was none of me left, not even for me. This way of life I had created had destroyed my person as well. I wanted to be the me that I was meant to be. The only problem with that desire was I did not know who that person was or even how to let that person emerge. Just how was I supposed to bring that person to the forefront? Just who was it that God had made before the formation of the world? What was it that I needed to do? This time, I wasn't willing to take the chance of messing my life any further. There had to be a better way of getting out of my own way.

What I needed was to be cleansed of where I was in my mind, in my thought process, and in my heart. I needed internally to look into my heart, and when I did that, I was unable to comprehend myself. Why had I made all the choices that had gotten me to where I was in my life? What reasoning had I used to justify myself for possibly ruining so many lives on the road to my personal desires? I was not willing to waste any more time on trying to figure things out for myself.

I had struggled long enough with suppressing the feelings I had about God and possibly what he wanted from me, but I was too afraid of how mad He was at me. I was too ashamed of how I had lived my life, and I was just in too much fear of what He would do to me because of all I had done in my life. It was a gripping fear that paralyzed my every move. How could I be afraid of the one who loves me like no other, the one who has given me the love that would fill my void? It was time to look somewhere else, other than inside of me, for answers. I needed Him to clean me, to look deep inside my heart and take out whatever madness laid waste there, and to pour His love in so that I could finally get some peace in my life and in my heart. *"The Lord has made all for Himself, Yes, even the wicked for the day of doom. Everyone proud in heart is an abomination to the Lord; Though they join forces, none will go unpunished. In mercy and truth Atonement is provided for iniquity; And by the fear of the Lord one departs from evil"*--Proverbs 16:4–6.

But just how was I going to bring that to life? What did I have to do to accomplish that internal feat?

* * * *

Enough Is Enough. Now there I was, reeling with anxiety about who I am, why I am, and where I am. I was sick of me. I couldn't seem to get out of my own way, as everything became a sore spot to me. No one was listening to me, at least it felt that way. I was spending more and more time alone, away from everyone, living with the failure of a life I had created, and I was more depressed than ever. And I hadn't yet stopped blaming everyone for my own problems. Even my acting out was no longer sufficient. I couldn't continue on this path; it had to stop.

Okay, so what am I going to do? I needed God, and I needed Him now, and it didn't seem like He was answering me. I felt alone and in despair, even away from Him. I began to be a very sad person, even more so than I had ever been, and I couldn't tell a soul. I just wasn't able to express how broken I felt inside. I couldn't tell the man I was married to because I had done some things that, I was certain, displeased him. So my last resort was to try to save myself, my family, and everyone from me. I was the common denominator. I had to go find the answers I needed.

I did not want to share myself with anyone else in this state of my being because no one was deserving of what I had to offer. My mind was telling me things that had me believing I was in it alone. How could I believe this stuff about me? So the only thing I could come up with was to get out, and after careful planning, I made my exit. And so the day came where I was ending yet another marriage. I was lost.

It was an unquenchable thirst for what I saw as my freedom from my own torment, making it one of the last things I was willing to do—have my freedom from my own pain. *"There is therefore now no condemnation to those who are in Christ Jesus, who do not walk according to the flesh, but according to the Spirit. For the law of the Spirit of life in Christ Jesus has made me free from the law of sin and death. For what the law could not do in that it was weak through the flesh, God did by sending His own Son in the likeness of sinful flesh, on account of sin: He condemned sin in the flesh, that the righteous requirement of the law might be fulfilled in us who do not walk according to the flesh but according to the Spirit. For those who live according to the flesh set their minds on the things of the flesh, but those who live according to the Spirit, the things of the Spirit. For to be carnally minded is death, but to be spiritually minded is life and peace. Because the carnal mind is enmity against God; for it is not subject to the law of God, nor indeed can be. So then, those who are in the flesh cannot please God. But you are not in the flesh but in the Spirit, if indeed the Spirit of God dwells in you.*

Now if anyone does not have the Spirit of Christ, he is not His. And if Christ is in you, the body is dead because of sin, but the Spirit is life because of righteousness. But if the Spirit of Him who raised Jesus from the dead dwells in you, He who raised Christ from the dead will also give life to your mortal bodies through His Spirit who dwells in you" --Romans 8:1–11.

* * * *

The Pain of It All. *"Woe is me for my hurt! My wound is severe. But I say, 'Truly this is an infirmity, And I must bear it'"* --Jeremiah 10:19. With every elevation of my work history, I grew in my own self-tolerance. And with every growth in my personal life, I became indifferent to others. Yes, my arrogance grew, and I am certain others saw it too. I would cut people off and out of my life at every turn and grew to feel as if my actions were justified because there was no stopping my growth.

I didn't feel that God was stopping me from feeling this way, always concluding God had given me everything I've always wanted in this life. I wanted to be a wife and mother and am that, I wanted to be a Marine and did that, I desired to work in an executive position and did that, I wanted to be a court reporter and am doing that. And there were so many rewards for those claims but many penalties and costs as well.

So as I sit on my bedroom floor, separated from my husband and family, looking at all the mail I had not opened, even dealing with the lack of food in my refrigerator, my pride winning this battle over my living life, there was nowhere to turn. I was alone. I knew I had felt despair before, but what I was feeling was quite different than despair; it was a feeling that I couldn't seem to describe. I had spent more time thinking about the feeling and the description of it than I did in any other type of living. I was gripped by it, literally unable to move, neither forward nor backward, not able to plan my future. Nevertheless, I existed with this pride, and I wore it like a badge of honor, which I had been awarded for destroying my family. The tug-of-war between the act of leaving my marital home and the feeling of gaining my independence back was yet another insurmountable feat. I couldn't even discern which feeling had the greater control over me.

And as I so proudly told anyone who inquired that I was tired of living this second-class citizenship and that I had been bold enough to say, "I was not taking it any longer," the reality of what I had done started to overshadow all the air of achievement. Needless to say, my whole world started caving in. It wasn't all at once but a quick process to the destruction of my world. I felt like God had served me up, but it was me who made the choices, me who planned and executed this path. I could not believe that God would do this to me, always being told of how He was a loving God. I convinced myself that He had to see my pain; He knew the torment I was suffering with and did nothing to stop me. But it all had to change.

Did serving Him mean it had to be this painful? I was believing a fallacy. The depth of my despair came from believing that the man I was married to, the church I attended, and the people I knew and had associations with were all opposed to me and that there was no hope for me. My thought was that I was going to find God for myself. *"You have shriveled me up, And it is a witness against me; My leanness rises up against me And bears witness to my face"* --Job 16:8.

I needed peace in my life, peace in my mind, peace in my heart, and peace in my everyday intent. My inward struggles were captivating for me personally, and I knew if they were this strong for me on the inside, they had to be visible on the outside. I had isolated myself from coworkers, church members, family members, my children, God, and almost totally my husband; and I could not seem to feel love from anyone. I was so convinced that the only person who could even dare to understand my pain was the one woman I had spent a lifetime trying not to be like, my mother. I had to learn to stop putting my will over God's will. But I didn't know how to do that.

It was a painful existence, and I had gotten to the point where enough was enough. I had to choose not to live with that kind of pain, but I did not know how to. I remember asking myself, *What did I do in my lifetime to deserve this treatment from these people? Was I really trying to fit into their scenario?* In awareness of my surroundings and after conferring with my own consciousness, I had determined that it sounded crazy and looked even crazier. Who were these people, and why would I care about whether I fit with them? Once again, I realized that I could not blame people I hardly knew and hold them accountable for my acceptance in this world. They were just doing what they do, them. I didn't fit into their way of life, hindsight being 20/20 to 40/40 to reality check, losing foresight the further I fell away. I wish I could go back to each one individually and thank them for the unwelcome positions they took toward me. Had I been accepted, I might be sitting in life right now with an oppressive point of view. So to all of those dissuaders, "thank you."

* * * *

So now this new life was in front of me, and I had to move through it, but I was not doing a very good job of it. In fact, I was doing the worse job ever. Talk about not being equipped for the next stage of your life. Well, I was there, and all I had to comfort me was my newfound freedom and no plans past that point. Oh yes, I had wild thoughts of what I could do once I was out of this nightmare of a life but nothing that I had put any footing under. As a matter of fact, what I did put footing under started to slide down a very slippery slope, with an avalanche behind it, and yet there was this little piece of me that just didn't seem to care how lonely I was. The lonelier, the better. I wanted everyone to just leave me alone.

It was then that I began to realize that my world was not in my hands once again. Had the Lord kicked me out of the driver's seat and put me in the backseat or the trunk? The fear of my new reality swarmed me. It was then that the gripping began to take shape. I had to send my son to live with his father because he was at the age of self-destruction, and my daughter was out on her own, and my job was the worst of it all; I had to work with people who seemingly took pride in being mean-spirited toward anyone who did not see things their way. I inwardly called myself Job. I felt served up, and I did not have any control to stop it. And then there was the bottom falling out. I felt no need to be here in this life.

My income dwindled down to nothingness. How was I going to pay bills with no money? I could only shake my head. I had to go into the savings that I had, that I was holding on to for dear life. It only lasted for about a few months, and then there was nothing. What in the world was I going to do, and who could I call for help?

I lay on my bedroom floor, crying to the Lord, screaming these questions at Him: "I thought you said you loved me. Why would you allow me to be like this? And tell me what I am supposed to do now. Where do I go?" So I cried myself to sleep every night and cried myself out of the bed in the morning, cried in the shower, cried in the car, cried to my mother on the phone, screamed at my ceiling as if the Lord was there, looking down on me from the ceiling, telling me, "I hear your cries and see your pain"; but I'm not ready to do anything about it right at this moment. I wasn't sure how to feel about Him, God, at this moment. I needed Him more than I ever have, but I felt as if He had abandoned me. My relief was not coming fast enough. How could I get God back in my life? I just couldn't figure it out.

I remember talking with my mom about my situation and my despair and not knowing what to do next. I needed God to tell me what step to literally take next, I needed Him to tell me what to think, I needed Him to tell me how to feel because there was nothing in me to muster direction, understanding, or any courage. I needed to move forward. I was stuck in my tracks. I felt like a boat in the middle of the ocean without an oar, motor, compass, or the ability to read the stars. I was alone, without my children, with no husband, with no job, and with no money; and every bill was behind and needed to be paid, and it was my secret. The only thing next was homelessness. I just couldn't tell those same people whom I had bragged about being out on my own. How could I tell them that I was destitute? I couldn't. And at some point, I even began not to tell my mother how bad it had gotten for me financially, emotionally, mentally, spiritually, socially. I was sinking further than I'd ever been before, and it felt like there was no way out. Yes, low was the order of the day, and it led me to thoughts of not needing to be in this life anymore. What was left for me? There was no one. I had come to the end of myself.

* * * *

Seeking the Answers. So even in this state of despair, I held on
to my childhood teachings of God never leaving you nor forsaking
you; just call on Him. But I thought I had been doing that the
whole time. Something was missing. How do I get to the point of
understanding what it was God wanted me to know? I needed the
kind of help only God can give. And I had never told anyone that
the only thing I did not have in my life was a relationship with the
Lord. This relationship would simply be my lifeline, the only card
I had left to play, my ace in the hole. So I played it.

While desiring a spiritual leader who could help me get to
where I needed to be, I asked the Lord in a statement sort of way,
"Lord, you know I want to get to know you, and I don't know
how to get there, so you're going to have to send me a spiritual
leader to help with clarity, someone who will venture to know me
and help me get to the place with you, where you want me to be.
Teach me how to walk with you" And so one day, I decided to go
back to church. I had no other alternative, except to live a life that
would not involve doing things I really did not want to do. What
I had truly wanted to do was to have a relationship with the Lord.
It had been one of my life's goals. I was tired of trying to figure
things out for myself while trying to fit that in at the same time.
I knew the Lord said that I should believe in Him and bring my
burdens to Him. I needed the Lord to take this weight off of me.
*"Come to Me, all you who labor and are heavy laden, and I will give
you rest. Take My yoke upon you and learn from Me, for I am gentle
and lowly in heart, and you will find rest for your souls. For My yoke
is easy and My burden is light"* --Matthew 11:28–30. This life had
to be easier than what I was making of it. My need for the perfect
life was the lie. It was a distraction from the truth.

Initially, it was an unlikely source who had given me the heads-up for the church, which would become my church home, just on a whim of a conversation. ***"I need to go back to church and stop playing with my life."*** It was just that simple. Out of all I had been doing that was not of God—morally, spiritually, and internally damaging myself—it had confounded me. I was tired of living according to my own thought or what my childhood dreams had taught me, but that I could be living a better life and having the truth of it all.

Knowing one of my core problems was trust, just how was I going to accomplish trusting anyone? It seems almost a waste of time to trust, and then the bottom drops out. People inevitably do what they want anyway. They want to talk to convince. I had to learn how to trust God first, and the rest would follow. *"Therefore do not worry, saying, 'What shall we eat?' or 'What shall we drink?' or 'What shall we wear?' For after all these things the Gentiles seek. For your heavenly Father knows that you need all these things. But seek first the kingdom of God and His righteousness, and all these things shall be added to you. Therefore do not worry about tomorrow, for tomorrow will worry about its own things. Sufficient for the day is its own trouble"* --Matthew 6:31–34.

I walked in the door of this church and heard the Pastor say, as the very first thing, that "this is a Bible-Believing, Bible-Preaching, Bible-Teaching church, and if you're looking for something else, you're in the wrong place." Was it said just for me? My soul felt a huge relief, feeling like someone had just taken the plug out. How could he know what I needed? It was creepy to me but in an "okay, Lord, you can't be showing yourself to me this quick" sort of way. I chalked it up to my own paranoia. It was a sensation that I had never felt before. All the while, I tried to maintain my cool; the inside of me wanted to jump up and down and run all around the church. It then went immediately to why the Lord did not direct me here sooner. He knew I craved these answers. *"For I do not desire, brethren, that you should be ignorant of this mystery, lest you should be wise in your own opinion, that blindness in part has happened to Israel until the fullness of the Gentiles has come in"* --Romans 11:25.

I had been periodically talking with my mom about the Lord and what I knew, and she would tell me what she knew, and we would always end in some type of disagreement. But little did I know that God had been working out more than one thing at a time. Although my mom and I had had a distant but connected relationship, it was always respectful but commanding. She had her demands, and I had mine. I was not going to be bullied. I had come to the understanding a long time ago that I wasn't in her shoes, and I did not know the things she had been through to make the decisions she made, so she was due the benefit of the doubt from me. She knew I was headstrong, but I don't think she knew just how much I was not willing to be convinced. I needed proof to believe more than what I already knew. *"While, through the proof of this ministry, they glorify God for the obedience of your confession to the gospel of Christ, and for your liberal sharing with them and all men"* --2 Corinthians 9:13.

I knew about Jesus and God because I was reared in church, but I had to admit to myself that I needed to read things for myself. I had always taken the word of preachers and others to stand in for me from the position of being a believer. But that just wasn't working for this situation. I needed answers, and the only way I was going to get what I needed was to do the work, open the book, and read for myself. And so I did but not at first.

I went to church every Sunday like it was a workday. I sat in the seat and crossed my arms. I was angry at so many things and so many people. I would see people that would come in just as I did every Sunday, and I would see how content they were, and I would say to myself, *If they only knew how destroyed I was.* I tried as best as I could to just pick up the same happiness they seemed to possess, but my inside waterworks never seemed to turn off. I felt like crying was a part of my being, and I couldn't stop.

I would sit and listen to the Pastor of this church so intently as if he was a life force between me and God. Remembering the words he was saying made so much sense to me. But there was one problem: as he would teach from the Bible and reference particular stories within the Bible, it seemed like everyone knew what he was talking about but me, and it was sickening to my stomach literally. I felt nauseated to know here is supposed to be the place of comfort, and I felt the least comfortable. Yes, I desired to fall into the arms of the Lord, and I wanted to feel everything would be all right, but I didn't feel that. I still wasn't sure what I was feeling, except contempt for myself because I was feeling so guilty for all my life's choices. It was a tiresome existence. I couldn't figure out the life I was meant to live. Why couldn't I put the puzzle pieces into place? The only problem with that was, what was the life I was supposed to be living? Was it a life I was to choose for myself, or how did God plan and see me living life? Just how was I supposed to manifest an existence out of this mess I was in?

* * * *

The Search Is On. I had to find out the answers to all my questions; so I pulled out the Bible, sat at my kitchen table, opened it up to the Genesis chapter 1 verse 1, and started there, verses that I had read many times and heard preachers teach on many times, but this time, I was looking for the meaning that was meant for me. Yes, I felt separate and special as I was growing up, so I drew on those special feelings, having those conversations with the Lord openly, out loud, in my kitchen at the table. I kind of felt lost in the amount of information that was before me. I felt a connection to the Holy Bible, but I did not understand it in its form. The only form I knew was the original King James Version, with all the "thees" and "thous," pretty hard to understand and get what I was looking for out of it. I needed it in plain truth. But the only problem with that was I was partial to that version and didn't want to trust any other version. I was fearful that a rewritten version of the Bible would somehow not be the same as the original one I had come to trust.

So as my Lord continued to reveal himself to me in this form of learning from this church's leadership, I began to take the classes in the church. I had to start to trust someone and/or something. And there was this wealth of information being disseminated at that time, and I wanted to get my portion of it. Would any of the information that was for me allow me to learn who I was worshipping and loving and counting on to spend my eternity with? The flood of emotions began to overwhelm me, and it brought a level of fear within me. It felt like there was an attack on my psyche. There was a weirdness to my emotional state, I confess. I was bogged down with all the ideas, theories, notions, stories, and beliefs I grew up with that I thought to be true, and I was beginning to question them all. I needed God to clear it up for me. I needed Him to let me know what to believe in.

It was a season of understanding for me. I was beginning to unfold my arms and relax a little when I went to church. I still felt as if I did not want to make friends because of prior experiences in church. I was not willing to put up with any nonsense. I had one goal in mind, and that was to learn all I needed to know to get myself out of this mess. I found myself preparing for church on Saturday as if I was going to school the next day. As my focus changed, my anxiousness became something else. It became awareness of my time and my space and my place. I began to become overwhelmed with joyful feelings I had about going to church every Sunday; it gave me such a peace. It was a small release from the anxiety and disappointment I had been struggling with. It was strikingly wonderful to focus on something else besides me.

I was not going to church for a position or because of family obligations or a husband or anyone else. I was going to church because of me and God, and it felt very, very good. It was something I was doing on my own. And not knowing anyone in this church at that time solidified my feelings of accomplishment. I needed to feel that I was making progress; it started me on my way. My personal and professional life hadn't changed with any significance, but I wanted to put this believing-in-God thing to the test. I started out feeling doomed and not needing to be here; there was no one to be here for. No one called, no one came, no one cared, so why was I living this life? For whose purpose did it matter that I breathed this air, struggling every day to feel the need to breathe? But I tell you as I sit here today, each Sunday I went to church, I felt slightly better about why I should be there.

It was a humbling experience to really believe that I was here for God's will, not mine. I had to stop putting my will above God's will. *"Good and upright is the Lord; Therefore He teaches sinners in the way. The humble He guides in justice, And the humble He teaches His way. All the paths of the Lord are mercy and truth, To such as keep His covenant and His testimonies"* --Psalm 25:8–10.

"Blessed be the God and Father of our Lord Jesus Christ, who has blessed us with every spiritual blessing in the heavenly places in Christ, just as He chose us in Him before the foundation of the world, that we should be holy and without blame before Him in love, having predestined us to adoption as sons by Jesus Christ to Himself, according to the good pleasure of His will, to the praise of the glory of His grace, by which He made us accepted in the Beloved. In Him we have redemption through His blood, the forgiveness of sins, according to the riches of His grace which He made to abound toward us in all wisdom and prudence, having made known to us the mystery of His will, according to His good pleasure which He purposed in Himself, that in the dispensation of the fullness of the times He might gather together in one all things in Christ, both which are in heaven and which are on earth—in Him. In Him also we have obtained an inheritance, being predestined according to the purpose of Him who works all things according to the counsel of His will, that we who first trusted in Christ should be to the praise of His glory. In Him you also trusted, after you heard the word of truth, the gospel of your salvation; in whom also, having believed, you were sealed with the Holy Spirit of promise, who is the guarantee of our inheritance until the redemption of the purchased possession, to the praise of His glory".

-- *Ephesians 1:3–14*

Hearing the reiteration that I was His creation and for His good pleasure, and hearing this being taught from a place I had begun to feel quite at home with, as well as having it shown in the same Bible I knew I believed in, God's Holy Word, I came to the conclusion that I could take the weight off of me and put it on Jesus. *Eureka!* Let's give that a try, which was a far cry from anything I was doing, since nothing I was doing was working. I wasn't quite sure how to put this belief system into play with total submission unto the Lord, but I had to believe that if I kept listening, I would soon find out. So I said to the Lord, "You said you came to save me. Okay, Lord, please fix me because I am broken." *"Have mercy upon me, O God, According to Your loving kindness; According to the multitude of Your tender mercies, Blot out my transgressions. Wash me thoroughly from my iniquity, And cleanse me from my sin. For I acknowledge my transgressions, And my sin is always before me. Against You, You only, have I sinned, And done this evil in Your sight—That You may be found just when You speak, And blameless when You judge"* --Psalm 51:1–4.

I was broken in so many ways that I couldn't even describe them all to myself. When I was growing up, I would hear quotes such as "By His stripes we are healed" and "God gave his only begotten Son that whoever believed in Him would not perish but have everlasting life" and even the 23rd Psalm, "The Lord is my Shepherd," but I did need the deeper meaning to it all and not just what it really meant on the surface. I found myself all over the place in my head. I wanted to know everything, and my appetite became voracious for all that I could stand.

I went to bed and slept with and woke up with my crutches every day. I was a disaster. I needed the despair to go away, I needed the anguish to go away, and I needed the guilt to go away. It wasn't that I liked feeling guilty; it was because it was such a feeling of loss that it was the only thing I could hold on to that I couldn't give away, nor could someone take away. How crazy was that? The things that were holding me down were the very things I wanted to keep just to have something of my own. They became my constant companions. My mind fed into them as if "we" were having a conversation day in and day out.

* * * *

Putting It in Check. So now we're in this unfamiliar place, knowing no one but desiring every bit of what it had to offer— family, unity, and understanding. It was just me in this place, with these people with the same goal. But while I sat there, I would say to myself, *Don't let them see you sweat.* Maintaining composure was what I did best. I did my suffering in silence, in the privacy of my home, with my door closed. I could not let them see me sweat. I could not let them know how bad things were for me, just how influential my internal struggles were over me. Imagining if they knew, what would they think of me? How would they treat me? How would they respond to me knowing my inner secrets, and can I stand up to the superiority that would come from them having that knowledge? Me, the great Marci, the one with this great professional life, the one who always maintained dress decorum, the one who always set herself apart from people, the one telling herself that she did not need them and telling them she wanted that fact to be known over all other facts. When, in fact, it was the exact thing I did need, I just didn't know how to go about getting it or even if it was an offering for me. *"For as we have many members in one body, but all the members do not have the same function, so we, being many, are one body in Christ, and individually members of one another. Having then gifts differing according to the grace that is given to us, let us use them"* --Romans 12:4–6.

I lived with the fear of being open and vulnerable. I just did not want anyone else to take advantage of me. I knew I was not strong enough to fight off whatever attacks might come my way. I possessed a hard outer shell, but my innards were just not prepared. Imagine, if someone were to split me open, all of the ugly fear, discontentment, and condemnation would have spilled out. Now we couldn't have that. I was so tired of living this way. I wanted someone to wake me from this nightmare.

I needed some lessons I had not had before. No, not those hard life lessons; I had had enough of those. I could have shared and given some of those away. I was talking about lessons of direction, lessons of humility, and lessons of clarity. I was so ready to put God into action. But that doubtful side of me wanted to prove Him wrong, that I just was not fixable, feeling I was too damaged and too broken, feeling I wasn't worthy of His grace. *"For this reason we also, since the day we heard it, do not cease to pray for you, and to ask that you may be filled with the knowledge of His will in all wisdom and spiritual understanding; that you may walk worthy of the Lord, fully pleasing Him, being fruitful in every good work and increasing in the knowledge of God; strengthened with all might, according to His glorious power, for all patience and longsuffering with joy"* --Colossians 1:9–11.

* * * *

Love Me or Hate Me. Now I knew I had "haters" but not that I was one of them. I was hating who God had made. I had come to hate the inside of me without truly knowing who that person was. Who was I in Christ? Who was Christ in me? Who was it that God made before He formed the earth? You want to talk about fear. Finding out who that person was, it was truly something I was afraid of.

Finding out who it was that God made would mean I would have to reconsider how I processed things, which means I had to put the end at the beginning. I had to adopt where it was I wanted to get to as my focal point. In other words, this time, I would put the horse blinders on for the journey. I would take out those worries, clear my mind of preconceived ideas, and try and get a handle on my wild, idealistic notions of how I saw life. Now this approach was just a little weird to me, just a little untoward because I really wasn't sure where this journey was going to take me. I had been in survival mode my whole life, and now I had to try to see the end and not worry how I got there. Although I did have the basics down, I wanted this deeper understanding, and I wasn't willing to settle for just any old story. I needed the back story, the meaning, the direction of it all, and the revelation intended.

I had asked the Lord for a spiritual leader, someone who would help me get the understanding of Him that I wasn't able to do myself, and He led me to this little church, the place where I shed my false pride. It is here where I got to ask the questions about the information I did have; it is here where I got to ask for the forgiveness that my soul was seeking and the direction that I needed. I wanted to trust with all that was within me and believe deeply that this is where my cleansing would take place.

Behold, had I known what God had in store for me on this journey, I would have taken it years ago. I soon found out that all that I thought I knew didn't begin to illuminate the depth and breadth of my Lord and Savior. The absolute humbling that I knew I had to do and wanted to do and craved to do easily began to win over me. I had to put myself in check and tell myself, *This really isn't about you.* And so I started with that question right there. Why isn't it about me? It's my life, right? *"In the beginning was the Word, and the Word was with God, and the Word was God. He was in the beginning with God. All things were made through Him, and without Him nothing was made that was made. In Him was life, and the life was the light of men. And the light shines in the darkness, and the darkness did not comprehend it"* --John 1:1–5. So as I sat and listened as intently as I could to what was being taught, I tried not to draw any notions of what it meant. I began to take it at a literal sense, which was sometimes good and sometimes not so good, meaning God was not playing with me. Yes, He did love me, *but* He was not willing to allow me to destroy my life and allow me to say He just didn't understand me while I did it, or He just didn't give me what I asked for that's why things didn't work out for me. But instead, He was willing to allow me to come to the end of myself and protect me in the process, while I would come to know what His Saving Grace was all about. And all I had to do was to allow the process to take control over my life.

It was a humbling experience, coming from one who strived for control over her every waking moment. It most certainly plagued the rationalization of me doing it this way. This tug-of-war was the greatest, but surprisingly, what aided in my lean from one side to the other was that I kept telling myself and anybody who would listen that God loves me, with such vigor I truly started believing it like I had been hearing it, like it was the very breath of my being. I said it so much that I felt that He just loved me and only me. It was powerful, cleansing, concrete, and concise; and as often as I said it, the more I believed it and came to feel it. It was the most connected to anyone or anything that I had experienced. *"Moreover whom He predestined, these He also called; whom He called, these He also justified; and whom He justified, these He also glorified. What then shall we say to these things? If God is for us, who can be against us? He who did not spare His own Son, but delivered Him up for us all, how shall He not with Him also freely give us all things?"* -- Romans 8:30–32 So I had to know more; I had to get it all. It became a hunger I initially I could not quench. Then there it was—classes, more study of the Lord, the answer to my thirst. And after loosening the grip I had on myself, I thought I would venture out. What could I lose by taking a class?

* * * *

"Are You greater than our father Jacob, who gave us the well, and drank from it himself, as well as his sons and his livestock?" Jesus answered and said to her, "Whoever drinks of this water will thirst again, but whoever drinks of the water that I shall give him will never thirst. But the water that I shall give him will become in him a fountain of water springing up into everlasting life."

—John 4:12–14

Taking the Drink. So as I thirsted for all that I could drink as though there wasn't enough and finding myself attracted to what could be possibly even more illumination because of every question that welled up inside of me, I was completely overwhelmed with the gift of Grace. Each time I questioned the understanding of what God was saying in His Word, the answers became clearer and clearer, with meaning and purpose. I couldn't get enough. And there it was, the time for my first class listed as Master Life. And I thought, *What, now I'm supposed to master the life that I have as a Christian?* I felt it was hard enough being me with the current set of rules I had to live by, and now someone's going to give me additional rules; there's no way was I going to even attempt someone else's way of thinking as to how and what I believe was God's direction.

Once again, I found myself fighting with my trust issues even more stringently. Why could I not break this perplexing feeling that somewhere someone would try and coax me into believing something I did not want to believe? It was part of me waiting for it to happen so that I could dispel all that I had consumed. I went in, thinking, *Protect yourself, don't give in, and don't believe everything they say as the Gospel.* I felt like I was starting all over again. I constantly asked myself, *What am I doing here?* but I kept proceeding down this path. And it was not a short-lived class. Actually, it was quite a long class, twenty-six weeks to be exact. And the first thing we did as a class was to determine whether it was going to be broken up or were we going straight through; straight through won out. So the ride was a long one, and I felt that committing to this twenty-six-week class was just what I was being led to do, and it was a way of showing even greater commitment to my growth in the Lord.

I set my mind to being back in a class. It was a wonderful feeling, allowing my brain to think about something other than work or whatever issues I had at home. It was a perfect way out, a way to be connected to something other than my pain. I initially felt drawn in, but when reality hit me, with all these different personalities applying themselves just as I did, I realized that it wasn't something I could do as a separate individual. I was taken aback at me having to participate and disclose just how much I knew or did not know.

I remember saying to the Lord, "Just how much of this humbling effect did I have to endure?" *"Humble yourselves in the sight of the Lord, and He will lift you up"* --James 4:10. It felt, at every turn, I had to once again humble myself to this process. Couldn't I catch a break and just be me again? Or was that what got me into this mess in the first place? Couldn't someone just give me the magic words or some magic pill so the fountain of understanding would prevail? Why couldn't it be that simple? Or would it be as it's always been in my life—having to take the difficult road, put in an extreme amount of work, question everything and everybody—before coming to point of contentment? And since I had already been struggling with this fear, which I had never had before like this, I became even more fearful of "what else I would have to change about myself."

But I just couldn't seem to shake the part of me that felt like an infant to the whole thing. I wasn't sure where to put those feelings of wanting my Heavenly Father to take me by the hand and lead me on(ward). Just lead me anywhere, other than where I was. Just because I had been attending church *every Sunday*, it doesn't mean that all those feelings that brought me back to church had dissipated. They were still present, always reminding me of my internal and external struggles. It was frustrating and exhausting. But in a quiet sense, there was this reassurance that I was heading toward solution.

This was another step to my evolution in Christ—learning my status of who I was in Him and He in me, learning the hierarchy of the Godhead, understanding the position we put ourselves in, among other things. These were all a part of this fountain. It was there for me to drink from it to be able to seek the understanding that I needed and to help me in such a way that my desperation soon began to subside. It wasn't an all-at-once sort of thing, but there were certainly moments that I drew on for the things that I needed to gain knowledge from. So I began to apply them to my every day. I guess it became like a remarkable dress rehearsal for me to be in a situation and then say, "Okay, Lord, let's see what you do with this madness." As I think back on my behavior then, now shaking my head at myself, I can just imagine that's what my Father in heaven was doing at me, just shaking His head with the comment, "Look at my child, testing me."

This period of learning had become what I'll call my situational growth. It was from all the reading, praying, and listening that I had done since my return to church that made me believe I was optimistically willing to apply this belief to my every day.

And just as those opportunities arose, I'd apply another one of God's principles to my living, and it was more than an eye-opener; it was illuminating. It began to bring forth a harvest for me, not the harvest of things but the harvest of faith, the harvest of trust, the harvest of belief. Each test provided an opportunity for me to call on God and see what he was going to do. I felt like I had been in a self-induced coma, and God had just healed me to wake me up, and everything was new to me. The world had changed right before my eyes, all around me, and I had to catch up. Only it wasn't the world; it was me.

I had gone from this hardened state of mind to faithfully believing that I didn't have to be the way I was any longer. My need to control lessened with every lesson. And the opposite effect was taking place with my belief system; the more I believed on the Lord, the more I sought Him out for direction with everyday living, the less I had to figure it out myself. Just what had salvation afforded me? *"Blessed is the man Who walks not in the counsel of the ungodly, Nor stands in the path of sinners, Nor sits in the seat of the scornful; But his delight is in the law of the Lord, And in His law he meditates day and night. He shall be like a tree Planted by the rivers of water, That brings forth its fruit in its season, Whose leaf also shall not wither; And whatever he does shall prosper. The ungodly are not so, But are like the chaff which the wind drives away. Therefore the ungodly shall not stand in the judgment, Nor sinners in the congregation of the righteous. For the Lord knows the way of the righteous, But the way of the ungodly shall perish"* --Psalm 1:1–6. What had my choice to follow Jesus done for the person I was or the person I was to become? And what should I do now with this newfound information? How was this going to affect me daily, if I truly give into the life as described in the Bible by Jesus, by the Apostle Paul, and by God? Could I affect the people around me? What was I to say to those I loved about the new me? How could I get these questions answered, and just where do I find the answers?

There was only one place, the Lord. And it would be the Holy Spirit, who is my counselor and guide, to lead me in the direction of fulfillment, enlightenment, and connectivity. I once again relied on the resources before me, the house of God, in which Jesus said that His house was a house of prayer and worship, and this had to be worship. *"Even them I will bring to My holy mountain, And make them joyful in My house of prayer. Their burnt offerings and their sacrifices Will be accepted on My altar; For My house shall be called a house of prayer for all nations"* --Isaiah 56:7. This had to be my commitment to the Lord. What else could it be? There was no name for it. I wasn't lost in my head because it felt complete. It was me, all me, wanting to get as much of the Lord as He was willing to give to me.

* * * *

Master Rules. So there I was—yes, there I was—poised to learn as much as I could. I mean, I was ready. I had set my mind to eight on the excitement scale, leaving a two for skepticism and truly not even knowing why I was skeptical. God had shown himself to me before, He had saved me, He had provided for me; but still, I was apprehensive. They were feelings that I had struggled with to the point of inner anger. I was angry with myself for feeling those feelings, when I believed there was truth yet to learn. This anger held another grip on me at every turn when I could not understand things. My first go-to was anger. But I knew little about what God had in store for me. It was an innumerable treasure. The wealth of discernible information was done just for me, or at least that's what it felt like. It was information I could understand. It was a course on living with the Master and becoming a disciple of Christ.

Yep, and I wanted to know what that meant. I wanted to follow Christ for personal reasons. I was sick of what this world was offering. I was determined to find out what it was God truly wanted for me. I had to know it completely, not partially or just enough to get by. I needed the backstory, what you don't always get in a two-hour church service. There is only a certain amount of time on a Sunday morning to get all that I was looking for, and this was the only way—additional classes.

This provided me with explanations for the myriad of questions, such as explaining the disciple's cross, the connection worship, service, praise, the Word, fellowship with other believers of Christ, and the dissemination of His message. It was exactly what my soul needed. I was a sponge; I sucked up every bit of it. It provided the scripture for every discipline—concise, exact, understandable; but it was hard work and a lot of it. I thought I had spent time in my Bible before, but my reading was nothing compared to the amount of reading it required. It was wonderful because the more I had to read, the more I found myself wanting to read, wanting to understand what I was reading. And it never let me down. It was an exercise in discipline, further growth, even more commitment. It had reached a part of my being that I felt was cast over for lack of attention—on my part, of course. It was reaching and had connected to a part of me that I knew my prior decision-making had set aside.

The choice of this class was a recommendation from my Pastor. It all stemmed from a discussion I had with him when I knew I wanted to seek additional instruction on the truth of what Christ was telling us. Yes, I had attended Bible study, and I had even attended Sunday school, but there is only so much time that the instructors have in answering questions. I knew how I saw the world and even how God had allowed me to see the world, and that was different than the average person. My views were analytical and detail oriented. I knew I always needed answers to everything—the "why" behind the event—and this was no different.

Why had God allowed me to have this perception? What was I supposed to do with this viewpoint? And this is where I found it out.

The breakdown and redirection of this view was wonderful because it had been exhausting standing on this ground seeing the world as crazy, that people had lost it, and that they had turned morally corrupt. It was a refocus of where Jesus was in all of that, and He has placed His followers in that as well, to bring forth His Gospel.

The class was set through four books of teaching: the understanding of picking up my cross as a disciple of Christ, what I was supposed to do with the mission of discipleship, how I was supposed to act within this engagement and commission, and what I should expect from the position granted to me by Christ. It had turned into a directional path that drew initial anxiety as I questioned myself as to whether I was capable of doing what Jesus wanted, still dealing with the doubt, still of little faith. What was I missing? I couldn't quite figure that out either. Was there a part of my brain that couldn't comprehend, or was I psychoanalyzing, scrutinizing, overprocessing every aspect of it, instead of building my faith to just believe what the Word of God said. I had to stop beating myself up over it. But I pressed on. I had to either figure it out or wait until God revealed it to me. *"Let a man so consider us, as servants of Christ and stewards of the mysteries of God. Moreover it is required in stewards that one be found faithful. But with me it is a very small thing that I should be judged by you or by a human court. In fact, I do not even judge myself"*--1 Corinthians 4:1–3. I had to believe in this way of life.

If you looked at my history and the decisions behind them, it was clear that I did not know what I was doing. The Lord's way had to be better, and it was just that—better. I had to give it time to work out for me. All that I believed in and all that was promised to me from God hinged on my devotion to it. It was going to take patience, just as He was patient with me. His long-suffering of my ways drew from my emotional state of respect, which I did not know I would have toward anyone. *"Our Father which art in heaven, Hallowed be thy name. Thy kingdom come. Thy will be done On earth as it is in heaven. Give us this day our daily bread. And forgive us our debts, As we forgive our debtors. And lead us not into temptation, But deliver us from evil. For thing is the kingdom and the power and the glory forever. Amen. 'For if ye forgive men their trespasses, your heavenly Father will also forgive you. But if you do not forgive men their trespasses, neither will your Father forgive your trespasses'"*--Matthew 6:9–15 KJV. It drew such a humbling posture that just the thought of it will immediately bring me to tears. And so working my way through this class, reading all the material provided, asking all the questions that I could muster and some that were self-explanatory, and even with a little turmoil with personality clashes, I stuck to it, and it was quite rewarding. It was so satisfying to feel the completion through choice and not obligation. What God had allowed in the form of truth through Jesus Christ was so satisfying to my soul that I told anyone and everyone of what God had done for me. It was an opportunity to converse with like-minded people and what we believed in, who we believed in, and why we believed it. And it was the Lord revealing himself through the art of lessons and through the lesson of perseverance, and the perseverance of God's love and perfect will was an exacting satisfaction. God defined it through Christ Jesus because He loves us so, and Jesus infused us with the right to it through Him.

* * * *

Biblical Selfie. Like clockwork, as soon as that class ended, there it was, another offering; and with just enough time between the first class and the second class, there we were at class number 3, Self-Confrontation. I would often ask myself, *Girl, what are you doing?* and yet loving every minute of it, so I pressed on into another extreme—yes, another twenty-three-week class.

Now it was this class that went into my true belief system. What was it I had been believing all my life? Self-confrontation was not about self-judging to condemnation but a realization between what was questionable and what was concrete. When asked why she was taking the class, one of my class members said, "To know what I know I know." Surety was the theme of the day. This was when viewpoint came into play. This was when the renewing of my mind became fixated on what it was God said overall. It was from day one, class one; walking into the class, the instructor had written on the white board, "What does God say?" profoundly justifying positional undertaking, clarifying positional viewpoints with evidence, and separating the lies from the truth. It was the Lord's stamp of approval on my belief system. It was my mark of definability. It was because there was no lead up to it; there was no comparing it to what everyone else said versus what God said. It went right to the point. It was immediately clear that we were not here for comparison; we were here for justification, sanctification, clarity, definition, and accountability.

The class started, and we went straight to the very theme of why were we there, and then we were off and running. The challenge began, which was to put it all into what it was God was really saying despite any preconceived ideas of what the world said about things or how the world wanted to interpret or reinterpret things, leaving no question to all I had learned in my lifetime.

So not only is self-confrontation a part of personal commitment but it also is essential for discipleship, as it teaches that four significant changes had to take place in my life: gaining a better relationship with God; divine empowering, which is always available by which to live the Christian life and on which I can now rely even more greatly; a new purpose for living, which is to serve my King; and a new plan for spiritual growth, which is to live by faith. It has helped me prepare myself for the approval by God, relate my conduct under the principles of Jesus's teachings of love, as well as help to restore others to victorious living, asking the question of who I am spiritually and what God calls spiritual. **Galatians 5:25 says that we are to "walk in the Spirit,"** meaning to live spiritually. It only matters if I am fervently following the

Lord. Let's not play here; straddling the fence is not going to work. I have to definitively choose a side. *"I call heaven and earth as witnesses today against you, that I have set before you life and death, blessing and cursing; therefore choose life, that both you and your descendants may live"* --Deuteronomy 30:19.

The struggle of letting go of what I thought was of Christ, and then finding out what the way to Him really was, was invigorating, to say the least, given that the Lord Jesus Christ is the rock upon whom everything for living is built. And although these topics were mostly taught in Bible-believing churches, I needed to concentrate on what I felt I misunderstood or I neglected or was taught under someone's reinterpretation of the Word.

As I truly put it into motion in my everyday life, living as my newly defined self and accepting this Christian lifestyle as defined by God, I had to learn what God granted believers as stated in 2 Peter 1:3: *"As His divine power has given to us all things that pertain to life and godliness, through the knowledge of Him who called us by glory and virtue."* What He said in His Word enabled me to do, according to 2 Peter 1:4: *"Escape the corruption that is in the world."*

Now just how does that manifest itself to me every day? I still want to catch up to the guy who's cutting me off while driving and push him over into a ditch. How do I get control over these deviant internal emotions that wants to drive me to immoral, illegal, and insane acts? To deny myself what haunted me spiritually would be to deny that I lived in an imperfect world. So why wasn't my world easier than before? I felt there was just a different set of rules to follow, but the madness was still available for the taking and accepting. And it seemed like the more I tried to separate myself from it, the more it was calling my name, knocking on my front door and just barging into my life.

I had to take a step back from new associations for a while, as well as depart from some old ones. The clarity that I needed for my every day was almost at a desperate state. I fought idealistically with my teacher in the class as much as one could and maybe even crossing the line of tolerance once or twice, but it was along with the instructor's never-ending obedience to God and willingness to put up with what I now see as my outrageous way of thinking, perception, and delivery; as well as my fellow classmates who challenged me to understanding.

We had a lesson one day on biblical dynamics of change, and as the chapter began to challenge us on how we saw ourselves on having failed to live God's way, it began to be the process involving putting off the old manner of life and putting on the new righteous practices in their place as stated in Ephesians 4:22–24, *"That you put off, concerning your former conduct, the old man which grows corrupt according to the deceitful lusts, and be renewed in the spirit of your mind, and that you put on the new man which was created according to God, in true righteousness and holiness."* Okay. So my question was how do I make that work for me now?

I really loved this class. I was poised with people who were not afraid to really ask tough questions and an instructor who was unyielding in his pursuit of delivery to what it was God said about any given situation, not for us to be theological about every situation but for us to be mindful of what it was we were instructed and directed to do and the way to live according to Jesus. It was the righteousness that now reigned in the forbearance of our living. It was without question what He intended for us. It was as the statement proclaimed, "God knows my heart." *"'Hear and understand: Not what goes into the mouth defiles a man; but what comes out of the mouth, this defiles a man.' Then His disciples came and said to Him, 'Do You know that the Pharisees were offended when they heard this saying?' But He answered and said, 'Every plant which My heavenly Father has not planted will be uprooted. Let them alone. They are blind leaders of the blind. And if the blind leads the blind, both will fall into a ditch.' Then Peter answered and said to Him, 'Explain this parable to us.' So Jesus said, 'Are you also still without understanding? Do you not yet understand that whatever enters the mouth goes into the stomach and is eliminated? But those things which proceed out of the mouth come from the heart, and they defile a man. For out of the heart proceed evil thoughts, murders, adulteries, fornications, thefts, false witness, blasphemies. These are the things which defile a man, but to eat with unwashed hands does not defile a man'"*--Matthew 15:10–20.

As a matter of fact, yes, He does know your heart. He knows every intent perpetrated by each desire. There is no getting away from it, either live according to the Word given to you or suffer the consequences. The truth of what His Word defines for us is already laid out, and it doesn't need redefinition. I am up against this world, but I have backup. I could live according to what He has laid out in His plan for me. It is divergent, but it is fruitful. He proclaims the connection that I was not alone in John 15:5: *"I am the vine, you are the branches. He who abides in Me, and I in him, bears much fruit; for without Me you can do nothing."* So what I have here is a definite new way of living, thinking, processing, and expectation.

And just how do I maintain this newfound dimension to my life? I was happier than I'd ever been, more joyful than I had ever been, but there were still parts of my emotional state posing as a constant conflict. I couldn't get past this notion of wanting to keep the Lord all to myself or not caring if others got it or not. It was blatant selfishness, and it drove me crazy. The inner battle or dominance over my emotional state and how I was to deal with my every day became my worst nightmare and my everyday prayer. What was I going to do about it? What was I supposed to do about it?

Here it was, preached from the pulpit put on the whole armor of God, with the definition and the scripture to go along with it. Ephesians 6:10–18 define it: *"Finally, my brethren, be strong in the Lord and in the power of His might. Put on the whole armor of God, that you may be able to stand against the wiles of the devil. For we do not wrestle against flesh and blood, but against principalities, against powers, against the rulers of the darkness of this age, against spiritual hosts of wickedness in the heavenly places. Therefore take up the whole armor of God, that you may be able to withstand in the evil day, and having done all, to stand. Stand therefore, having girded your waist with truth, having put on the breastplate of righteousness, and having shod your feet with the preparation of the gospel of peace; above all, taking the shield of faith with which you will be able to quench all the fiery darts of the wicked one. And take the helmet of salvation, and the sword of the Spirit, which is the word of God; praying always with all prayer and supplication in the Spirit, being watchful to this end with all perseverance and supplication for all the saints."*

There was only one word for it, "tangible."

* * * *

It was the cleansing blood of Jesus Christ that has allowed my understanding of who I am. And certainly with other classes and other studies, coming to understand the covenants and where I was in time and space, it all fell tightly into place. I was in the Body of Christ; my name was written in the Lamb's Book of Life. I was at home and awaiting my home to come, which was not of this world but with my Lord and Savior. He offered it and I accepted it, just as He has accepted me. My fate and my place are solidified, and I am so thankful.

REALITY CHECK

REALLY. And so it was put plain and simply to me in a reality sort of way, and that way was simple, once you think about it; I could not go around doing anything I wanted in this life without damaging myself if it wasn't the way of the Lord. I had had enough picking and choosing what was appropriate and then expecting the Lord to fix my messes for me.

I couldn't take freedom of choice as a badge of discord and explain it away as if it was my free pass to accept the things this world was offering as truth and then try to put a biblical ribbon around it and present it to God as if it was a gift from me, and He now had to accept what I was offering him yet still save me from it when it wasn't working in my favor. I couldn't continue judging this world to condemnation, blaming all for why I was in the situation I was in.

My freely accepting what the Lord laid out for us was profound. Removing my thought process and replacing it with the Word of God is my constant teacher. I now know I have the answers I have sought out to live life.

Life is for the living, so I thank God for waking me up from the dead.

THE OFFERING

So as Salvation came as an offering from God, with the freedom of choice that He sent through His Son, born of a Virgin, who came through the House of David as proclaimed in **John 3:16:** *"For God so loved the world that he gave his only begotten Son, that whoever believes in Him should not perish but have everlasting life."*

And so the pinnacle of why Jesus came was to do his Father's will, which was to offer Salvation as extended in **John 3:17:** *"For God did not send His Son into the world to condemn the world, but that the world through Him might be saved."*

Therefore Jesus taught us that the way of reconciliation is through Him as He said in **John 14:6:** *"I am the way, the truth, and the life. No one comes to the Father Except through Me."*

THE REVELATION

Romans 12:1–2 said, *"I beseech you therefore, brethren, by the mercies of God, that you present your bodies a living sacrifice, holy, acceptable to God, which is your reasonable service. And do not be conformed to this world, but be transformed by the renewing of your mind, that you may prove what is that good and acceptable and perfect will of God."* And it was those verses that propelled me into the common sense of it all. It was my mind that was having the struggle and that was being attacked, not my moral sense of things. I knew right from wrong; it was my choices that chose the path. It wasn't my understanding of where I wanted to be spiritually because I didn't possess the lack of commitment toward it, and it wasn't my desire to want this natural way of life.

I always believed there was heaven and that it was with God that I wanted to be, and so that meant coming to the decision that I wanted to walk with God, like Enoch did. If I desired a place with God, I had to find out how to get there, and He explained it.

It was through His gentle mercies that I had to renew my mind to what He wanted of me and for me—offer my body as a living sacrifice, holy and acceptable to Him—and that meant I had to make that mental change. I wanted my head to follow my heart, since my heart had always belonged to the Lord. And since I always saw things differently than most people, this transformation only made sense to me. Why would it be so hard to pick up my cross as Jesus said in Matthew 16:24? *"Then Jesus said to His disciples, if anyone desires to come after Me, let him deny himself, and take up his cross, and follow Me."* It was a perplexing thing to me at first since I did not know exactly how to do that and how that would actually manifest itself to me today. What did I have to do to pick up my cross? I've learned that it is as I do everyday things as part of my life, His will, according to His Word.

So it was clearly how I saw the path of it all. Not always having total control over myself and the lack of understanding is what brought me to my decisions in life. It was not always what someone had done to me because they did not always have control over me. There was no gun to my head. Weakness, fear, blame, and guilt kept me from having direction, and that direction was to the King of kings. Because once I asked for that whole healing and I came to believe that I did have faith and I needed to strengthen that faith and most importantly that I was a child of the All Mighty King, and that He does love me and that I shouldn't expect to live less than because that's not what He gave me to believe in, it was on; that thought process became me, I became it, and it was what I stood on as my belief.

And although it was not an easy place to get to, it was daunting sometimes and an overwhelming experience, only because I wasn't expecting to understand it the way I have come to; it was exactly what the Lord has said, coming from darkness into the Light. I used to hear people say that my entire life, and I thought, *What was the big deal?* Cut the light switch on. Clearly, I did not have sufficient knowledge of what it meant to be in the dark. *"For you were once darkness, but now you are light in the Lord. Walk as children of light (for the fruit of the Spirit is in all goodness, righteousness, and truth), finding out what is acceptable to the Lord"* --Ephesians 5:8–10.

And since I had always attended church, either through childhood rearing or other relationships, it never occurred to me that there was a distinction that coming into the light meant that it wasn't just something for me here on this earth, that it was also something that was going to propel me into my relationship with the Lord. *"Do not lay up for yourselves treasures on earth, where moth and rust destroy and where thieves break in and steal; but lay up for yourselves treasures in heaven, where neither moth nor rust destroys and where thieves do not break in and steal. For where your treasure is, there your heart will be also"* --Matthew 6:19–21.

It had always been just a part of my nature to believe that I was going to be in heaven with Jesus because all I had to do was believe that He was sent from heaven and that He was the Son of God and that He ascended back to the right hand of the Father. This was my childhood understanding from a very young age. I knew I loved God, and I understood that Jesus was God's Son and even knew of the Holy Spirit, but there wasn't a true understanding of the Deity and of His Sovereignty. He said, "I am that I am." I got that. Your Word reigns over all. *"Therefore let that abide in you which you heard from the beginning. If what you heard from the beginning abides in you, you also will abide in the Son and in the Father"* --1 John 2:24. But coming to know Him as my Heavenly Father and that I could have a relationship with Him, see Him as that—my Father—and call on Him as that, it has taken some progression of revelation, and that brought me to the point of acceptance, repentance, forgiveness, and reconciliation so that I could begin to ask questions now freely, without reservation, and lovingly and excitedly waiting for answers from Him. It has taken a lot of questions for me to get to the point of now looking for God to work in my life, and it has given me great joy to sit back and see what He's going to do next.

* * * *

I asked a simple question on the subject of Communion and was then showered with a direction, which easily matched the greatest thing I've ever learned, for it is my communing with the Lord that makes my relationship with Him.

Now back in church, again, serving on the Lord's Supper Committee just wasn't good enough, I needed to get a better understanding of what it all meant, taking Communion. It was God's revelation of Himself to me that led me to my relationship with Him; it led to my prayer life with Him, it led to my relationship with Jesus Christ as well as with the Holy Spirit, and it has led to my total communing and being one with Him. It has been an experience like no other. *"I communed with my heart, saying, 'Look, I have attained greatness, and have gained more wisdom than all who were before me in Jerusalem. My heart has understood great wisdom and knowledge'"* --Ecclesiastes 1:16.

"For I received from the Lord that which I also delivered to you: that the Lord Jesus on the same night in which He was betrayed took bread; and when He had given thanks, He broke it and said, 'Take, eat; this is My body which is broken for you; do this in remembrance of Me.' In the same manner He also took the cup after supper, saying, 'This cup is the new covenant in My blood. This do, as often as you drink it, in remembrance of Me'".
--1 Corinthians 11:23–25

* * * *

God has allowed me to come to know myself and know the things of my heart so that I can see my life and understand this life, from the places in my heart that bring love behind them, instead of seeing life from the places that had affected my emotional state, from the place of anger or disappointment or guilt. God allowing me to know Him from a place of love and acceptance and salvation and not from a place of begging, loneliness, and desperation. The thankfulness I possess for this grace from God has afforded me to accept the things I cannot change and the courage to change the things I can and the wisdom to know the difference, living one day at a time; enjoying one moment at a time; accepting hardships as the pathway to peace; taking as He did this sinful world as it is, not as I would have it; trusting that He will make all things right if I surrender to His will so that I may be reasonably happy in this life and supremely happy with Him forever and ever in the next.

I am so thankful I am no longer seeking to please the natural things that would be considered gods to some, such as money, position, someone/anyone to love me. I am His, and He is mine, and He loves me, and I love Him. I am at His feet, acknowledging Him as my God, my Lord, and my Savior; loving that He put his Holy Spirit inside of me as a constant guidance and comforter and that I'm standing on His promises; knowing that He will never leave me or forsake me; and also knowing that I will have life's challenges but that I have Him.

I am welcoming of the challenges in my life but knowing that He has already taken care of them for me and that I can go through those challenges, watching and waiting to see what He's going to do. Yeah, it might get ugly at times and seemingly unbearable, but it's where I am at my weakest that He is at His strongest. This life of mine was a plan of His. He predestined my path and let me live this life that He gave me. He tested me and then gave me a testimony; because He brought me back from the brink of insanity, fixed my broken vessel, dwelled within me, stood me up, dusted me off, sent me out with a mission, equipped me to do the job, blessed me in my obedience, and has loved me the whole time, and His love continues.

Lord,

I thank you for my life.

* * * *

Psalm 34:1

The Happiness of Those Who Trust in God

"I will bless the Lord at all times; His praise shall continually be in my mouth."

JOY

"But the fruit of the Spirit is love, joy, peace, longsuffering, kindness, goodness, faithfulness, gentleness, self-control."

--Galatians 5:22–23

"Now may the God of hope fill you with all joy and peace in believing, that you may abound in hope by the power of the Holy Spirit."

--Romans 15:13

PEACE

"Peace I leave with you, My peace I give to you; not as the world gives do I give to you. Let not your heart be troubled, neither let it be afraid. You have heard Me say to you, 'I am going away and coming back to you.' If you loved Me, you would rejoice because I said, 'I am going to the Father,' for My Father is greater than I."

--John 14:27–28

FAITH

Now faith is the substance of things hoped for, the evidence of things not seen. For by it the elders obtained a good testimony. By faith we understand that the worlds were framed by the word of God, so that the things which are seen were not made of things which are visible."

--Hebrews 11:1–3

"The Lord is my light and my salvation; Whom shall I fear? The Lord is the strength of my life; Of whom shall I be afraid?"

--Psalm 27:1

LIFE

* * * * * * *

Life is a gift. Don't begrudge it. Take it, accept it, and be grateful for it.

But consider Him the life raft.

Picture yourself in the middle of the ocean without an oar, compass, or stars to guide you home; and someone sees you, comes to save you, throws you a life raft, and pulls you out of the water. You are forever grateful.

That is what this gift of life is, which God gave us, a vast ocean and the exploration of it. But He sent his Son to save us from drowning within ourselves and this life of sin. We should ask for the raft (salvation), take it, accept it, use it, and be forever thankful for it.

And most importantly, give honor to the giver and the deliverer of the raft for loving us enough that He would send the raft to save us from drowning, for it is that loving-kindness that saves our lives and brings the Gift of Life to us through the Raft.

Jesus is Lord, and He Reigns as the King of kings.